Praise for *The Naked Opus*

"Chris Delaney's *Naked Opus* reveals the true nature of wealth by stripping away the idea that we are alone in our journey. He reminds us that the true measure of wealth is found in living a purposeful, collaborative and connected life—to family, friends and to our own humanity. A thought-provoking, original classic that will surely change lives and the very meaning of wealth itself."

> —*Tom Deans, Ph.D., Author of* Every Family's Business *and* Willing Wisdom

"*The Naked Opus* is game changing. It adds a new dimension to the wealth management story by demonstrating to advisors how to authentically listen to their clients' goals to provide solutions that are deeply resonant. A must-read for all investment professionals and their clients."

> —*Carol Fickling, Portfolio Manager, Wealth Advisor & Financial Planner at RBC Dominion Securities*

"I just loved it! *The Naked Opus* is well conceived and is a practical story to which both clients and their advisors will relate. It was a great way to spend a Sunday afternoon."

> —*Carol Foley, Lawyer and Chartered Professional Accountant*

"*The Naked Opus* reveals the *evolution* of estate planning and is timed perfectly as there is so much intergenerational wealth about to transfer. It asks advisors and families to dig deeper and really articulate what wealth means to them and what they are hoping it will mean to their future generations."

> —*Rebecca Griffith, MBA, FICB, Small Business Consultant, BexBiz, and Mortgage Agent/Advisor, Streetwise Mortgages*

"I can see *The Naked Opus* being mandatory reading for families starting the discussion of family wealth transfer, or for advisors, such as lawyers and accountants, trying to get into the field of intergenerational wealth advisory services."

—*John Neretlis, MBA, CHRP, FEA, Next Gen Anesti*

"Clients are sophisticated. They deserve advisors who are at the top of their game and who embrace modernization. The time has come for advisors to work in collaboration with with one another, ego aside, in order to discover the true values and goals of our clients. Chris cleverly illustrates essential, progressive ways of being of service to families through his storytelling, in a book that takes us through a journey of growth and inspiration."

—*Nathalie Boutet, Family Law Lawyer, Mediator, and Certified Family Enterprise Advisor*

THE
NAKED
OPUS

GROWING YOUR FAMILY WEALTH
FOR THE LONG TERM

CHRIS DELANEY

MILNER &
ASSOCIATES INC
· EDITING · PUBLISHING · COMMUNICATIONS · CONSULTING ·

ISBN 978-1-988344-01-0 (paperback)
ISBN 978-1-988344-02-7 (e-book)

Production Credits
Editor and project manager: Karen Milner
Copy editor: Lindsay Humphreys
Interior design and typesetting: Adrian So, adriansodesign.com
Cover design: Adrian So, adriansodesign.com
Printer: Friesens

Published by Milner & Associates Inc.
www.milnerassociates.ca

Printed in Canada
10 9 8 7 6 5 4 3 2 1

To my whys, Hannah, Adelaide and Jennifer

Contents

Foreword   ix

Introduction: The Naked Opus:
             Growing Your Family Wealth for the Long Term   1

Chapter 1: A Need for Change   13

Chapter 2: Purpose   37

Chapter 3: Building a Better Way:
             Communication, Values and Mission Statements   65

Chapter 4: The SMRT Strategic Engine   103

Chapter 5: The Abundant Estate in Action   141

Chapter 6: Aligning the Advisory Team   163

Chapter 7: Purposeful Wealth   181

Chapter 8: The Naked Opus   203

Epilogue: A World of Abundance   221

Endnotes   225

Acknowledgments   226

Public Speaking and Additional Copies   227

About the Author   228

Foreword

I HAVE KNOWN CHRIS DELANEY for a number of years and he and I share a similar background and journey. We both started our careers as practicing lawyers and we both became impatient with the lack of solutions the legal system offered our clients.

Case in point: I met a seventy-three-year-old retired professional whom we can call Ben. Ben had $15 million in the bank, but had not talked to his children in years, hardly ever went out, had no friends and no hobbies. His conversations were always about investments, taxes and interest rates. Ben, a prisoner of his wealth, rarely left the house. In his will Ben said there should be no announcement of his death and no funeral ceremony. He did not want to leave money to any of his children "for reasons they know of."

In quantitative measures Ben was wealthy, but in qualitative—intellectual, social and human—terms Ben was bankrupt. Strange as it seems, there are so many antisocial behaviors caused by wealth that there is a word for it: *affluenza*. Affluenza is defined as:

The unhealthy and unwelcome psychological and social effects of affluence regarded especially as a widespread societal problem, such as: feelings of guilt, lack of motivation and social isolation experienced by wealthy people.

Ben may be an extreme case, but affluenza is a widespread affliction in today's society, affecting people in every life stage: children, teens, young adults, parents and grandparents. Particularly susceptible are high-net-worth individuals and their families. In fact, affluenza is only one symptom of a much bigger problem: the inadequacy of traditional planning to preserve family wealth.

Today's approaches to managing and planning for family wealth focus primarily on the financial assets; paradoxically, planning only for the money and the distribution of assets in an estate is a direct path to destroying family wealth within three generations. With trillions of dollars set to pass from one generation to the next in the coming decades—the largest wealth transfer in history—this is a growing concern. Chris Delaney's vision offers a more holistic planning paradigm that can not only preserve family wealth more effectively, but also grow it for generations to come.

The Naked Opus not only tackles the problem of affluenza, it offers us a fresh new approach to planning for the family legacy—one that has abundance at its core, not merely the distribution of assets; one that focuses on growth and not just preservation; one that engages multiple generations with the wealth, rather than dividing them; one that brings strategy and purpose to the table, not just tactics.

Although Chris Delaney no longer practices as a lawyer, he is one of the more thoughtful estate practitioners in North America. He is also very sensitive to the human condition, an Olympic-caliber listener and a very effective questioner. Now he has written a book that every estate, tax, insurance and wealth advisor in North America and beyond should read and then give out to their clients.

Chris is deeply troubled and deeply concerned by the state of wealth and estate planning today, typified by a 2015 article in the *National Post*, entitled "How to keep your kids from blowing the family fortune." The article cites a research survey showing that 70 percent of families with net worth of $3 million or more lose that wealth in the second generation. The survey showed that:

- 78 percent feel the next generation is not financially responsible enough to handle the inheritance
- 64 percent admit they have disclosed little to nothing about their wealth to their children

The survey lists various reasons: People were taught not to talk about money, they worry their children will become lazy and entitled and they fear their financial information will leak out. This attitude is not surprising considering that these families are advised that everything about their wealth and income must be kept confidential.

This advice comes from the traditional legal, accounting and financial professions. Most professionals understand the enormity and extent of the affluenza problem but very few question it. Most assume that the only way to protect wealthy families is through legal documents and litigation.

These traditional professionals primarily emphasize their technical prowess, their understanding of tax rules, accounting standards or economic issues. Talking about emotional issues is for the weak and less competent, they say, and how can you justify billing for that? Technical issues are where the money is.

Worse yet, the legal system is designed to prevent change. Legal analysis is based almost entirely on "past precedent," we are ill-equipped to try anything innovative or revolutionary. As a former trial lawyer, I acknowledge that the legal system can change through legislation, but it is so incremental that from a big-picture perspective it is almost unnoticeable.

That traditional mind-set no longer works in an environment where disruption is the norm—in the economy and in society in general. In an age of disruption, where there is so much wealth at stake, it is clear that we can no longer be restricted only to the solutions of the past, that we need new large-scale solutions to deal with the issues we face today. The luminaries among us, like Chris, are shaking up the status quo with new approaches to planning and new ways of looking at wealth.

Chris has done a masterful job in conceiving and writing *The Naked Opus*. Written as a novel, it tells the story of Rick Gilmour, an estate lawyer who recognizes affluenza as a solvable problem and carefully designs a process to avoid it with careful strategic planning. As engaging and easy to read as the story is, don't let the spoonful of sugar fool you. This book delivers the medicine. The care and work that went into designing each of the conversations is obvious. And the innovative solution and fresh approach that unfolds in its pages will be infinitely helpful to advisors as well as to clients and their families.

The Naked Opus brings vision, structure and purpose to the planning process, yielding the potential of deeper engagement and more positive outcomes for all involved. After reading it, I will approach my own facilitation engagements in a more confident, purposeful manner and I am sure you will too.

John Mill, LL.M.
Author of *Hire Your Buyer: A Philosophy of Value Creation*

Introduction

The Naked Opus

Growing Your Family Wealth for the Long Term

SEVERAL YEARS AGO, I was working with some families on their inter-generational succession planning. The engagements were typical: a series of discovery meetings followed up with planning suggestions to be shared with their other professional advisors. The recommendations I had made were largely technical in nature to avoid and minimize tax at death, to provide a trust structure for young beneficiaries and to consider some risk-management tactics in the event of a calamity such as becoming legally incompetent. The typical stock-in-trade of the estate-planning lawyer.

These clients were always grateful for my professional perspective, but I sensed that something was missing from my process and output. Personally, I felt my suggestions lacked authentic relevance for the client. They failed to resonate on an emotional level. The ideas were technically sound, but I found it very difficult to be enthused about saving a few dollars on tax at death or about ensuring a simple and efficient distribution of assets to avoid probate tax. The suggestions were hollow and lacking in purpose. Of course, tax minimization and disaster planning are both critical imperatives, but I couldn't escape the sense that they had become the only considerations driving my advice to these clients and others.

At the conclusion of one especially memorable engagement, the client seemed unsettled. The proposed solutions were very efficient and saved her family a great deal of tax cost. Trusts were suggested to protect the wealth until the beneficiaries reached adulthood. She was extremely polite and expressed satisfaction at the various technical solutions provided; however, her body language and half-smile revealed that she was clearly seeking something deeper and more profound.

"You seem unhappy with this process," I commented, a bit confused by her reaction.

She paused, still looking down at the paper, and responded, "No, no. This is all very informative and you have gone to so much effort. It will save my heirs a great deal of money and frustration."

I sensed this wasn't the honest truth and that she was too polite to say what she really meant. And so I asked her, "What did I fail to address? It's okay," I assured her. "I need to know."

After a moment of nervously fumbling with the edges of my report, she lifted her eyes and answered, "How do I get this wealth to my family?"

I was thunderstruck. I stared at her for a moment and realized I had been asking all the wrong questions. I had a checklist in my head through which I was very efficiently scrolling. I assumed taxes were a concern, and I assumed she would be interested in risk-management considerations. The process had become about my needs rather than hers. I realized that I had asked the questions *I* wanted to ask rather than endeavoring to meet her where *she* was and discover the questions *she* wanted answered.

I put my pen down and pushed my papers to the side of the boardroom table.

"Oh my," she said softly. "I have offended you."

"No, no . . . not at all. You have done me a huge favor, actually," I told her.

"Well, I didn't want to interrupt you as you did all your work," she said. "I mean, what do I know about this? You're a lawyer; you're the expert and I'm sure you have done this a thousand times."

"That may be the problem," I laughed. "Let's start again. Is that okay?"

"All right," she nodded.

"What's the worst thing you can see happening with your financial wealth? What must we avoid at all costs?" I asked her.

She reflected for a moment and responded that she was worried it would be damaging to her family; that it would destroy their entrepreneurial spirit, motivation, civility, ambition and connection. She was curious about how her financial wealth could be deployed to enhance and nurture her family. Not once did she mention tax. Not once did she mention the financial threats of divorce or bankruptcy.

I realized her goal was to use the financial wealth she had created in a manner that would continue the growth into successive generations of her family. She wanted to be generative with her wealth and invest her financial capital *into* her family so that it could propagate growth well into the future. She wanted to make sure it lasted as long as possible in order to provide the maximum level of opportunity to her heirs and maintain her family's core values. She believed, although she didn't quite know how to say it, that her wealth was imbued with purpose that transcended its simple exchange value. Similarly, she didn't view her estate planning as a transaction or a technical moment simply to transition assets, but rather, she saw it as part of a lifelong process of intergenerational wealth creation and stewardship. She suspected more clearly than I that my initial plan would create disengaged, ungrateful, unprepared and narcissistic heirs. This was not the family wealth legacy she envisioned for her loved ones.

This was a turning point in my professional thinking. I eventually realized that this client's planning needed a strategy that was focused on sustaining her core values and goals—goals I hadn't taken any time to unearth and fully understand. I hadn't made the effort to give definition to the true sources of her wealth and her objectives for it. She wanted to make sure the wealth survived her children and her grandchildren. She wanted her family to view her financial resources as a source of capital to invest in creating dynamic traditions and innovative potential for generations to come. As such, while it was vital to ensure that the core wealth wasn't dissipated before it reached the rising generations, it was far more important that the money be purposefully deployed *into* the existing beneficiaries. She turned my planning paradigm on its head. Instead of simply planning for the protection of the financial wealth, she also wanted to prepare the heirs to successfully receive the financial wealth.

Finally enlightened, I took time to research her goals and satisfy my own lingering desire to acquire a more profound vocabulary and robust intellectual model for client engagement. I came across a body of work centered on avoiding the phenomenon of "shirtsleeves to shirtsleeves in three generations." This old adage, common to many cultures around the world, captures the all-too-common experience that wealth in most forms is created by one generation, stewarded by the next and squandered by the third. People go from nothing, to wealth and then back to nothing in three generations. This was at the core of my client's concern: How can we avoid this entropy effect on wealth? How can I turn a moment of loss caused by death into a moment of creation and continuous opportunity? How can I build adaptive skills in the rising generation to achieve these outcomes?

I believe that current intergenerational wealth-planning models guarantee that the entropy effect on wealth will continue between generations for several reasons:

1. The planning is focused almost entirely on tactical solutions, such as tax minimization, being the main reason for the planning. However, effective planning starts with clear goals and ends with tactics.

2. Purpose, vision and goals are rarely considered in the planning. As a result, the outcome lacks any emotional or strategic value.

3. Planners fail to take a genuinely holistic and interdisciplinary approach to their efforts. They provide technical advice within the silo of their expertise.

4. The process of creating a purposeful and growth-oriented intergenerational wealth model demands a lot of hard work,

time and patience. It goes places that can be difficult, such as complicated family dynamics. Many families and their advisors aren't interested in that depth of commitment.

5. Finally, and possibly because of the prior reasons, it suits most advisors and clients alike to focus almost exclusively on the family's financial wealth and ignore the longer-term efforts needed to sustain the broader bundle of family wealth, including intellectual, social and human capital, across many generations. They adopt short-term tactics rather than invest in long-term strategies.

This book is about improving the various outcomes of estate planning by creating an authentic and strategic process and embracing a generative, values-driven mindset that avoids the "shirtsleeves to shirtsleeves" paradigm. In the process, a more strategic and purposeful relationship with total family capital is created. This relationship results in a broader view of family wealth in terms of its components and its potential to be self-sustaining. Indeed, I am of the view that the estate-planning process is best practiced not as one of entropy-inducing tactics but, instead, of strategic family wealth creation.

What is family capital or family wealth? It's actually much more complex than just the money. To keep things simple, I include four main components:

1. **Financial capital**—the dollar value of the real and financial assets of the family.

2. **Intellectual capital**—what the family knows and, importantly, includes the stories told from one generation to the next.

3. **Social capital**—the collection of relationships the family and its members enjoy in the community.

4. **Human capital**—what makes each person in the family uniquely worthy and valuable.

In an enterprising family, where a multi-generational business is present, these various sources of capital can even create competitive market advantage. In every case, the admixture of these and other potential sources of family wealth, such as moral or spiritual capital, creates a multiplier effect on family wealth that results in the sum of the whole being greater than the individual components.

In the context of these multiple types of capital, the process of creating your estate plan is a great deal more than simply transmitting financial assets from one generation to the next. It is certainly that, but it also includes an opportunity to use your wealth plan to propagate and nurture the other forms of wealth—to make them generative. Viewed in this manner, estate planning becomes a life-long process and not a one-time event simply targeted at the point of death.

A central proposition of this book is that people should invest their financial capital into the development of the other three forms of family capital to ensure a successful wealth transition. In this way, the financial capital is used to nurture, educate and develop heirs to make them good beneficiaries. When you invest your financial capital to enhance the social, intellectual and human capital in your family, you in turn increase the chances of your financial wealth being sustainable over many generations—potentially an endless virtuous circle and a meaningful, lasting legacy. This fuller and more holistic approach to wealth and estate planning is an essential first step towards minimizing the risk of a "shirtsleeves to shirtsleeves" experience. It is a process of investing in and preparing your heirs to be servant-leaders and stewards of generative family wealth for their own heirs.

• • •

Investing financial wealth into the broader wealth of the family is fundamentally a strategic process. It demands clear and authentic goals, driven from articulated and shared values, that are put into action through various strategies and tactics. The process is not well-served by starting with the tax planning and other technical issues.

Instead, it begins with discovering and understanding the purpose behind the planning. This process is time-consuming and demands effort from all of the participants—advisors, clients and their family. It's also difficult work that requires a commitment to curiosity and a willingness to function within a multidisciplinary framework. However, the rewards of sustaining wealth, preserving family relationships and choosing purposeful, integrated plans are substantial.

To make the process work, you need to clearly articulate, and then thoughtfully advocate for, your goals and desires. You need to be informed and understand what is possible. You must ask questions and probe deeper when given an unsatisfying response from any advisor—not a technically unsatisfying answer, but a strategically hollow response. You must become an advocate for your own planning rather than a passive consumer. It's not the advisor's estate plan, it's yours; it's your story that is being written and not theirs. The process revealed in this book will help you become a successful advocate for your own planning needs.

Purpose and vision are unique to every person and, by extension, every family. Understanding the vision requires a deep dive into the heart of the family's values. Every family member will have independent values that frame the choices he or she makes in life. Most people don't bother to identify, discuss and prioritize those values. Most families don't make any effort to share those values to identify common threads for strategic planning. However, to be successful with intergenerational wealth transfer, families must be willing to shed their veneer and reveal these core elements. It is only by getting naked in this manner that a shared vision and mission for family wealth can be established.

Lawyers, investment advisors, private bankers, accountants, insurance professionals and other advisors have access to a wide variety of tactical techniques in order to implement an estate plan. However, any plan that lacks strategic cohesion, authentic governance and an effective communication model is doomed to repeat the "shirtsleeves to shirtsleeves" experience. People planning their wealth transfer must accept the effort and challenges that are required to give full effect to the process. You are crafting a story that will be told and retold for many generations after your own death. It is the work of many lives and experiences that creates a beautiful and dynamic intergenerational work of art—your family's opus.

Revealing and creating your own core story, or naked opus, is a strategic process. If the family wealth is intended to be enduring and self-promulgating, or generative, then that process of planning must be imbued with purpose. It must be purposeful in order to have deliberate meaning and impact on others—your family and loved ones. It cannot simply be an event characterized merely by simple-minded tactics. This is a proven recipe for wealth entropy.

In this book, I have suggested a process that has five specific steps you can take to build your own purposeful plan. There are many ways to execute on these five steps, and I only illustrate a few. The important thing is to acknowledge that it is a process and build a plan that works to achieve your own unique needs.

• • •

The Naked Opus is intended to help readers engage their estate planning as an ongoing and growth-oriented process. The five steps will generate a family wealth plan that builds capacity for ideation, creation, adaptation and long-term sustainability. It doesn't mean it will happen, but the environment is enriched to allow for the possibility.

The process, which I call the "Abundant Estate," has five key components:

The Abundant Estate

1. Begin a process of having family meetings to address the various topics for your intergenerational wealth planning.

2. Use a meeting cycle to discover and articulate your shared family values.

3. Use a meeting cycle to create a family mission statement based on the shared family values.

4. Utilize a SMRT strategic process:

   a. **S**uccess in the achievement of the mission is made possible by identifying key personal and family goals.

   b. **M**eaning is brought to goals by setting clear objectives to break the big goals down into smaller, achievable steps.

   c. **R**ecipes for action are established when strategies are created to achieve the objectives.

   d. **T**hings that will be done to execute on the strategy are tactics.

5. Assess the professional advisory services needed to support your strategic intergenerational wealth plan and assess the strategic capacities of your current professional advisory circle. Once revealed, take the steps necessary to fill any gaps.

This process has the benefit of being a virtuous circle of good planning. Every step enhances the previous aspects of the planning while building towards strengthened and sustainable outcomes. It creates collective and individual growth mindsets that are curious, generous and purposeful. These qualities add the missing "A" throughout the SMRT strategic process: adaptability. A curious mindset is an adaptive mindset. Purpose changes with altered internal and external forces. The capacity for adaptive flexibility is essential for multigenerational success. It turns a good plan into a truly smart one.

The first four steps are the very core of the process. They are intended to spark an ongoing engagement and a passion to plan. Many commentators and white papers suggest that as many as half of North American adults don't have any type of will plan. In my experience, this isn't a surprising number. I see many wills that are drafted but remain unsigned; the client feels the document is unsafe to formalize because they fear it will create certain and immediate havoc in the family. In other cases, the client doesn't want to own the unknown consequences of the plan. Either way, having no will puts intergenerational family wealth at profound risk for destruction.

Moreover, and just as dangerous, many existing plans lack any cohesive strategic approach to the transition of the wealth between generations. They are minimalist documents that simply shepherd financial wealth to the beneficiaries in a tax-efficient and expedient manner. No effort is made to consider the goals, potentialities and expectations of the beneficiaries. No effort is expended to understand the broader sources of family wealth and engage the financial wealth to support the intellectual, social and human wealth of the family. The consequence of this kind of planning is that wealth is destroyed very quickly as it passes between generations. This incomplete approach to planning causes the total family wealth to decay through entropy.

The fifth and final step in the Abundant Estate process is about having advisors who work as a high-functioning team and not exclusively within their own professional silos. It's about ensuring cohesive advice that supports your own process by adding strategic value in addition to simply implementing tactics. Authentic process coupled with aligned and values-oriented advisors is a powerful planning proposition. Unaligned advisors, just like unaligned family members, are like a rowboat with oars on only one side. You expend tremendous resources to go in lots of circles and get nowhere better at the end of the process.

This book uses a narrative format to reveal the Abundant Estate process. The characters and situations are entirely fictional; however, I have tried to use advisor perspectives as much as possible to show, in a composite manner, how different advisors approach the same client problem. The idea is to draw all parties out of their silos and into a better experience. My hope is that this will allow any reader to connect on a personal and emotional level with the characters and their situations.

The main character, Rick Gilmour, is an estate-planning lawyer working outside the traditional practice of law as a planning consultant in a wealth management firm. In addition to collaborating with internal and external lawyers and accountants, Rick works with investment professionals and others who service clients of the firm. He has a unique perch from which to observe the estate-planning experience for most people. The Abundant Estate model is revealed through his interactions with peers and his own personal development journey.

The Naked Opus is not a technical book and is not intended to be constrained to specific jurisdictions or professions. It is intended to help people to be advocates for their own planning and to understand that they won't get what they want unless they expend the resources of time and some treasure to discover what's most important to them. For advisors, using the Abundant Estate approach will help you develop deeper and more meaningful relationships of trust and abundance with your clients.

I could have added a sixth step called "Get Going!"; however, my experience and my hope is that this step will be unnecessary to state. Once family members are committed to walking this path, they will be excited to continue the journey commenced by reading this book and to begin exploring and revealing their core values and goals in order to create a powerful family narrative—their very own naked opus.

Chapter 1

A Need for Change

"For time and the world do not stand still. Change is the law of life. And those who look only to the past or the present are certain to miss the future."

—John F. Kennedy

THE PHONE RANG at Rick's desk a little earlier than normal. It was late summer and most people in his office were on vacation. He was already calling it the year without summer. It had been cold and overcast most days and many of his fellow office workers had delayed their vacations hoping for some good weather. Seeing none in the forecast, and with Labor Day looming in a few weeks, people started to take time off anyway and hope for the best. As a result, the office was peaceful and distraction-free.

Rick was in early to prepare for some upcoming meetings. A lawyer by training, he had exited the world of private legal practice to provide consulting services for the clients of wealth management firms, mainly on estate planning and business-transition planning.

On this mid-August morning, he was reviewing wills, powers of attorney, trust deeds, shareholder agreements and financials for two upcoming meetings with business-owner clients he would be meeting for the first time. It was not unusual in these meetings to be peppered with tax-related questions, and this required some basic familiarity with the clients' existing structural planning. Rick preferred to use the initial meeting simply to get to know clients a little, but it was better to be prepared in case the client had different expectations.

As he reviewed the Hartmann file, he was struck by the vintage of the documents. "Yikes. Lionel Hartmann is at least seventy-five years old," Rick thought to himself as he reviewed the will. "And his will is well over twenty years old."

Putting down the will, he picked up the shareholder agreement for Hartmann's business, Savage Communications. Savage was a large regional Internet provider and there were several family and non-family shareholders. Rick started at the back of the document to determine the signature dates and was horrified to see the document was never executed.

He shook his head and made a meeting note: "Ancient will, no shareholder agreement." Rick was more disappointed than surprised to see the planning nightmare that was ready to unfold if Lionel suddenly became incapable or died.

He continued to read the contents of the Hartmann file and make notes to remind himself of questions he needed to pursue. After a while, he set that file down and began to sift through the Patel file. He read the trust deed and the wills. He also examined the corporate financials for Noora Patel's cosmetics distribution company. She had three children and a very modern family situation. Her oldest two children, a son and a daughter, worked in the business. Her son, Anil, was divorcing and had three young children of his own. Aashna, Noora's only daughter and the oldest child, was the operations manager and had trained as an accountant. Rick didn't know much else about them but he was curious that the youngest child, Raj, was excluded from the power of attorney documents and the distribution of the company assets.

"Uh-oh," he thought to himself. "Somebody's in the doghouse. There may be some bad feelings in this family."

After noting several questions to ask about Raj's exclusion, Rick flipped to the executor appointment section of the will. He was stunned to observe that Anil and Aashna were trustees on the business will. Worse yet, perhaps, was that all three were co-executors of the non-business will. He wrote to himself: "Ask Noora if she had considered the potential for family strife in this appointment scheme." Thinking about his question, he decided to add "!!!!!!"

In three coffees, also known as two hours, he looked up from his desk and saw through the windows that a pretty nice summer day seemed to be shaping up. "It's sunny out for a change . . . maybe I can get out early today and head to the beach with the kids," he thought. He put his head back down into his files and resumed his work.

By noon it was dark and rainy, and Rick thought to himself, "#stupidsummer." He realized that with the advent of Twitter, he now placed mental hashtags on thoughts as they occurred to him. Laughing to himself, he promptly took his iPhone out and tweeted that very thought. Technology had changed the language and communication system of entire generations, including his own.

He opened up his calendar and glanced ahead a couple of weeks. He was getting very excited about attending "Convergence," an upcoming conference in California hosted by the Summit Institute for Family Wealth Planning. Rick had sought out this conference after several recent client engagements had left him professionally dissatisfied and curious to identify a better approach to intergenerational wealth planning. The breaking point had occurred after one client in particular had politely endured his current boilerplate process and review of his report for almost an hour. Rick had proudly identified many tax savings and efficiencies to avoid probate. However, he noticed that the client, Claire Usher, seemed unsettled.

"Claire, are you satisfied with these observations and suggestions?" Rick had asked her.

Claire shifted uncomfortably in her seat and offered effusive but hollow thanks. "Oh yes," she started to explain. "My children will save a great deal on fees and taxes, and the whole process should move along tickety-boo. Not that I will be around to enjoy those joyous outcomes."

He had laughed a little at her sarcastic comment then put his pen down and paused for a moment to reflect on the juxtaposition of her gentle manner and the stinging critique. He didn't deserve the kind words. He hadn't been successful in reducing her planning fears one iota.

He waited a moment and then asked, "Claire, what were you really hoping to achieve from this process? What did *you* want to see happen? What was the burning question *you* wanted to resolve?"

She smiled and then responded, "I thought you were never going to ask. Actually, I really wanted to know, how do I get this wealth to my family?"

As if a bolt of lightning had struck his thick skull, Rick suddenly understood that Claire was concerned about how her financial wealth would impact the lives of those she loved the most. She didn't care about taxes much, and speeding up the estate administration seemed a hollow victory for her at that juncture. She wanted to know how she could enrich her family rather than damage them with a sudden influx of financial bounty. She didn't want to plan for her money, she wanted to plan with purpose for her family.

Rick suddenly appreciated that he had been planning for her estate as he wished it to proceed rather than digging deeper to understand her values, goals and motivations.

Claire, who seemed to notice that Rick was having an epiphany, politely let him sit quietly for a moment. When the dead air became too extended, she gave a slight cough and said, "Ahem."

Waking up, Rick answered, "Claire, I'm sorry. Your question is so elegant and profound. I think I understand where we were disconnected. I really think I made some big assumptions and relied too much on my checklists and routine planning. I focused almost immediately on the 'how' of your planning before I understood the . . . ."

"The 'why,'" she interrupted with a smile.

"Can you share with me how this came to be such a concern?" Rick asked.

"Well, as you know, I come from an entrepreneurial family," she began. "The source of our family's financial wealth came from an inheritance from my grandmother, Mabel."

Rick interrupted apologetically, "I actually had no idea. That was a question I didn't ask. I just started from where you are today. I showed no curiosity at all."

"Let's ignore that and start fresh. It's exciting, this is the first time I have ever shared this story with an advisor. So, we are already breaking new ground," Claire smiled.

Rick was thankful for her grace.

She continued, "Mabel left a sizable fortune to my mother, my aunts and one uncle. In that era, it was enough to provide a life of relative leisure. My Uncle Jake and his family played their cards that way, and it was a disaster. The money was all gone by the time my cousins finished high school. Well . . . the ones who went to high school."

"They were just sitting back in life and waiting for the money?" asked Rick.

"That's right," Claire replied. "They are a hardscrabble lot and they managed in the end. But they truly wasted the wealth and had much tougher lives than needed to be the case. But what really broke my heart was how unprepared my Aunt June was for the money. She seemed afraid of it and lived an unhappy life hoarding the wealth and fearing everyone's intentions. She trusted very few people," finished Claire, with deep sadness in her voice.

Rick was staggered at the rich tapestry of stories that adorned Claire's relationship with financial wealth. He had never asked clients these types of challenging questions before. He wondered to himself, "How have I missed these great stories around wealth? These intergenerational experiences are incredibly powerful and deeply ingrained. People have stories to reveal and understand. By ignoring these moments, what kind of advice have I been giving people?"

To Claire he said, "So your concerns for your own family and financial wealth have a real history. A mixed bag of experiences. What would you like to do differently?"

"I don't like the randomness of the experiences," she told him. It's not healthy in the family. I want there to be more purpose to things . . . more purpose in the planning."

The two then chatted at length about the deeper concerns and goals Claire had for her loved ones. They agreed at the end of that session to meet again in a few weeks to address Claire's real concerns.

Driving home from the meeting, Rick grasped that he was desperately in need of a better model or process for his service. His tried-and-true approach was simply no longer satisfying or robust enough for his more thoughtful, purposeful clients. The world was changing in all sorts of ways and it was time to change how he engaged with and planned for his clients as well.

After much Internet research and a referral from a friend, Rick had discovered the Summit Institute for Family Wealth Planning. Members of the Institute included lawyers, accountants, family business advisors, wealth consultants and financial services professionals who seemed to share his emerging planning values.

Looking in his calendar now, he was pleased to be reminded that the group's annual collaborative conference, "Convergence," was only two weeks away.

Suddenly, a giant crack of thunder and flashes of lightning startled him out of his introspective daydreaming. He was saddened that the nice summer day was shot now, and he put his head down to work. "San Diego can't come fast enough," he thought to himself as he waded into yet another report filled with tax advice and probate planning suggestions.

• • •

Around 1 p.m., Rick stood up and stretched. The rain was falling heavily now and, having forgotten his umbrella, there would be no walking to the coffee shop for refreshment. He was stuck in the office tower until quitting time. He took the elevator to the food court and grabbed a black Kona coffee and a muffin. As he finished paying, he saw his good friend Dave Milne sitting with others having lunch.

"Dave! How are you?" asked Rick as the two men exchanged handshakes.

"Rick, it's so good to see you," said Dave. "I'm just here today with some new clients. Rick, this is Kim and Tom Skinner. They own the local food markets Always Fresh around the area."

Rick extended pleasantries and accepted their offer to join them while they finished up lunch. After a few minutes, Kim and Tom excused themselves and headed to the parking garage to return to their head office.

"They are really nice people," said Dave. "I wish all my clients could be so progressive. Now tell me, Rick. The last time we chatted, you were making some changes in life. How is that project going?"

"Couple more weeks and I'll be attending the Convergence conference. I'm really excited," he said.

"Any concerns?" asked Dave.

"What do you mean?" asked Rick. "Concerns? It's a conference. I think it will open my eyes to some new planning ideas. It should make me better at what I do."

"Five years ago I started having doubts about the work I did for clients," said Dave, who was also a lawyer but still in private practice. "I started to research some different elements of planning, attended two earlier 'Convergence' events, and ended up writing my book," he continued.

"I give that book to almost all of my business succession clients. It's a great read," added Rick.

"Thanks, man. The problem was, it forever altered how I see the world and how I engage my clients. It triggered a complete change of service paradigm. I can't ever go back. I see the planning process very differently now and it makes me a bit of an outlier. Are you ready for a tectonic shift in how you do things?" asked Dave.

"Well, I guess," said Rick. "I mean, I really view it as an addition to the work I do. Another tool in the toolkit."

"If you're going, don't go half-assed," advised Dave. "Go all-in when you get to the conference, and soak it up. I know some of the folks you'll see there and will likely start to interact with. It might only be an add-on to your present service model, but my guess is it will be transformative. You need to be ready. Are you ready?"

"You're freaking me out here a little, Dave. Ready for what?" asked Rick.

"It's possible that you won't approach a client's file the same way afterwards," said Dave. "When you return, what seems typical and ordinary today will look pedestrian, self-serving and tired. That's what happened to me. I started to develop engagement models that were very different from my previous practice. Some clients loved it, others weren't sure what was going on. I also changed my whole billing structure, moving away from hourly billing. I started to attend conferences that were about networking and building communities in this field. Other lawyers started to see me differently. I lost some clients but gained many more new ones. It was exhilarating but scary at the same time. We are early days on this approach to planning."

"Hmm . . . ," said Rick, taking in what his friend had said. "I suppose I should expect the possibility that the changes are more than minor. Most of the time, conference experiences are the same. You know, update on this and potpourri of that."

"It will be what you make of it," added Dave. "The work you do will change, and some clients and advisors won't know what to do with it. People don't respond well to things they don't understand or that threaten their own world view." He checked his watch and said, "Speaking of which, I have to meet the Skinners' accountant right now."

They promised to chat again soon and Rick headed back up to the office. He hadn't really considered the possibility that the path he was on would be such a quantum shift.

Entering the office, he could hear his phone ringing. He raced around the edge of the desk and grabbed it. "Rick Gilmour," he answered.

"Rick, it's Teresa. How are you?"

Teresa was a lawyer with a similar role to Rick's, but she worked on the west coast.

"Doing okay for an old fella," Rick replied.

Teresa laughed and asked, "Are you planning to attend the National Lawyers Conference in two weeks? We were looking at the list of attendees and your name was absent. Did you forget to register?"

He chuckled and answered, "Nope, I didn't forget. I am going to a different conference this year. A non-technical conference. I have been looking forward to it for quite a while," he said.

"Non-technical? What about your continuing education credits? Will it satisfy those?" Teresa asked.

"I don't really care," Rick told her. "Some of my learning requirements will certainly be satisfied, I suppose. It is an estate-planning conference after all. I am using holiday time and I've paid for the conference registration myself. It's an adventure."

"Why would you bother to do that? Did you try to get it paid for by the company and they said no?" she asked.

"No. I didn't even ask. I was pretty sure I knew the answer in advance. They had rejected an earlier request for a similar bit of training, so I could see how the stars would line up on this one. It's okay, though. It will be great," Rick said, quite happy to hear himself say this to his colleague.

"Well, I still don't get that," said Teresa. "Why spend your own money and do something that doesn't enhance your technical skills? You're odd sometimes, Rick. Look, the real reason I ask is that Marcus can't attend the NLC because of a family emergency. He is taking a leave and they wanted to fill the spot with someone from our team. That's when they noticed you weren't registered. Serena is likely to call you and ask if you want to take it so they aren't out of pocket. Just a heads up," she added.

"Thanks for the alert, but I'm already all booked for my Convergence conference in San Diego, so no can do," laughed Rick.

They said goodbye and Rick resumed his paperwork until 3 p.m., when the phone rang again. Rick could see from the call display that it was his manager, Serena.

"Hi, Serena," he answered. "How are you?"

They talked for a few minutes about family and the miserable summer. Serena then got down to the point.

"Did you hear about Marcus?" she asked.

Rick pretended he had only heard a rumor and let Serena fill him in on the details. He asked that she please extend his thoughts to Marcus at this difficult time.

"Can you take his spot at the NLC?" she asked.

"I'm using a few vacation days to attend another conference at the very same time. I am sorry, but I can't," he said. He explained the nature of the conference he was attending and was surprised that she started into a full-court press to try and convince him to take the NLC spot instead of attending Convergence.

"Look, we have paid for that spot for our team and it would be great if you can take it. I kind of thought you would already be going. It's ideal for you; I don't quite understand this other content you want to take. How does that add to your value proposition for our clients?" she asked.

"Well, it's something I have wanted to do for a while and I have some vacation planned around it," he said, not willing to yield.

"Well, maybe can you get out of it and go next year? I could pay for it next year maybe? I can't promise that, but I could try. Otherwise, I lose the NLC spot to another team. I might not get it back in my budget next year. I appreciate you have other plans but if you can escape them, it would be a tremendous help," she pushed.

Rick said he would think about it and let her know the next day. He had a cancellation window on his hotel and was quite certain the flight could be altered at nominal cost. Serena seemed to have the impression that he would make the needed changes, but he wasn't sure at all.

Sitting at his desk after the call, he felt a little uncertain. He decided to text Dave and see what he suggested.

He started the text conversation:

Rick:

Hey, boss wants me to sub in for NLC instead of
Convergence. Colleague had to bail. Thoughts?

About twenty minutes later, Dave responded:

Dave:

Did you check the NLC agenda? Anything you need to
hear? Anything that will be transformative with respect
to the work u do?

Rick had already looked at the lineup and was only mildly inspired.
It was the usual fare of tax updates, legislative updates, case law
updates, tips and traps and best practice offerings. All were vital to
maintaining his level of technical proficiency, but he had already
attended events on many of these topics in the past year. There was
nothing really exciting or new. He texted back to Dave:

Rick:

#meh The usual fare. No, nothing I *need* to hear.

After a few minutes:

Dave:

Are you ready to wait a year to attend Convergence?

Rick thought about that. If he didn't attend it this summer, he would
have to delay the experience an entire year. Normally, he would put
it off. But something, including his recollection of his recent meeting
with Claire, was telling him Convergence was going to be transfor-
mational to his work and he needed to attend now rather than a year
from now. He texted back:

Rick:

U know what, I'm not.

Dave:

Don't swap out. But they will be confused
and u may pay for it.

Rick realized that was possible. If he rejected the offer to attend the
NLC, he was sending a message to the firm about his priorities. He
decided to think on it and call Serena in the morning.

• • •

The next day, after a surprisingly restless sleep, Rick called Serena to advise her that he had given it some additional thought and he really preferred to stick with his initial plan. He was sorry that the NLC spot might have to be used by someone outside the team, but he was really quite invested in the choice to attend Convergence.

"I get that you have a vacation booked around it," Serena responded. "I'm sorry if it seemed like I was putting the pressure on, I am getting some myself. I don't really get the conference you're going to though," she added, noting that she had checked it out online the night before. "I mean, you're a subject-matter expert, how does the content at Convergence add value to the conversation with clients? It looks sort of like soft-skill materials to me. You know, touchy-feely," she queried.

"Well, I have traditionally thought the same way," Rick told her. "But my sense is that those soft issues, if left unresolved or made worse through inadequate planning, result in litigation. That's a hard cost, in my book."

Rick remained steadfast and would not take the NLC spot. Serena was clearly frustrated but nothing worse. She seemed pleasant at the end of the call and he was hopeful that would be the end of the discussion.

Later that afternoon, he received a text from Dave:

Dave:
Did u cave in?

Rick:
Nope, stayed firm. Close call though. LOL.

Dave:
Good choice. More tests will come but you are on a path now.

Rick:
What, am I on the road to Mordor?

Dave:
More than you know.

• • •

Rick glanced at his phone and saw that it was 5 p.m. He had a late-day client meeting to attend upstairs. Just then his e-mail chimed with a note that the clients were about to arrive in fifteen minutes. He was asked to come up and get some background facts on the situation. Rick zipped up to the boardroom to meet the advisor, Liz Stowe. He was surprised to observe that the clients' lawyer was also present for the meeting.

Rick introduced himself to the lawyer, Ben Dower, and made some light conversation. The solicitor was much older than Rick and had a general practice. The clients, Carol and Mark Gumble, were described as former business owners with some liquid wealth since the sale of their operation. Their two children were adults, and there were grandchildren. Rick was provided with wills, powers of attorney and two years of personal tax returns. He was also given the financials for the post-sale investment holding company.

"It's pretty simple really, Rick," began Ben.

Just then, the Gumbles entered the boardroom. Everyone exchanged business cards and small talk until it was time to get started. Liz thanked the Gumbles and Ben for attending. She also introduced Rick and his role.

"We have done a lot of planning already and I am pretty sure this is more of a review than anything," interjected Ben suddenly. "It's all been vetted through their accountant and it is solid post-mortem planning. The tax bill is as low as we can get it. Carol, Mark: I got here a little earlier and so, in the interest of time, I gave Liz and Rick the lay of the land."

"I would agree that it looks very efficient," said Rick. "Ben, I hope you don't mind if I ask a few additional questions of the Gumbles. I like to understand the motivations, goals and thoughts that go into the process," he added gently, and as he did, he glanced at Carol who was looking like she, too, had some questions to ask.

"Oh yeah, no problem. Ask away," said Ben.

Rick looked at Carol and Mark and asked a few questions about things such as dates of birth and citizenship. He commented that he was jealous they had already retired while they were still so young and vibrant.

"Oh, we are not retired at all. We just sold the business Carol started because we had concerns about the business cycle we were in. We're just getting started. Carol is only sixty, after all," laughed Mark.

"My apologies. That's even more exciting. What business are you going into?" asked Rick.

"We travel a lot and buy fun stuff while we are abroad. If we really like the items we acquire then we try to arrange to sell the products online. It's so much fun we may make it a bigger business. It's still a baby for us, but we are always going to be entrepreneurs. Why stop? To do what? Golf all day?" added Carol with a chuckle.

"Was that on the agenda when you sold the retail stores?" asked Ben. He seemed a little startled to learn they had gone right back into business. "I mean, I seem to recall that you said you would travel the world on your investment returns from the sale when we last did the wills."

"Well, Ben, that was six years ago. A fair bit has changed. We got bored and then our vagabond daughter, Emily, started Millennials Against Malaria. She travels the globe and we decided to carry her luggage," laughed Carol.

"It's the only way we get to see her," added Mark.

Rick spent a fair bit of time getting information about their children, Emily and Sera. Sera was married to Carl. They had two young children and lived on the west coast. Emily was single and spent most of her time raising money from foundations and working in the third world with other non-governmental organizations. Sera was a school teacher with substantial child care expenses. Emily had no particular use for money. It was a situation that was both modern and fraught with planning and family-dynamic complexity.

"I noticed that the wills leave all the wealth to the girls equally. How do you feel about that now, six years on from making the last will?" asked Rick.

"I have some concerns about what happens to the grandkids if Sera and Carl get divorced after we die. They are okay today, don't get me wrong. But I worry about that possibility. I also worry that Emily would give it all to charity and then be a pauper in retirement. It's all good not to care about money when you are young and healthy . . . but she may never earn much. How will she live when she's older?" asked Mark.

"Well, you can't rule from the grave, Mark," said Ben. "They're adults. If they haven't learned to manage wealth by now, it's hard to see how that will change much. You just have to trust what you have taught them. I rarely suggest trusts because they are complicated and expensive."

"Is that fair to say?" Carol asked Rick. "I mean, I have heard that before, and we likely aren't rich enough to use trusts, anyway."

"That's likely right, Carol," Ben interjected. "I have been doing this for thirty-plus years now and what we have in place is what most of the clients in your situation do. It's pretty standard. Plus, it's very tax-efficient. This was something you wanted."

"I have organized your investments to minimize probate tax at death as well," added Liz.

The Gumbles nodded appreciatively. The turn of the conversation towards tax minimization seemed to comfort both clients; however, Rick noticed that Liz was making extensive notes and seemed unsettled by the focus on taxes and simple efficiency.

Rick smiled and continued, "I noted that the girls are named as co-executors. However, Sera lives quite a distance from here and Emily is very often abroad. Is that something you wanted to explore a little further? I mean, it may be a challenge for them to work together, and the distance won't help much. Is this still viable? How well do they get along?" he asked.

Carol and Mark looked at each other and Rick knew there was an issue.

Ben jumped in and said to the clients, "Well, the reality is that a lot can be done by Internet these days and they could simply use an agent like me or another lawyer from our firm. There really isn't anything to fight over; it's fifty-fifty and they are adults now. It's their duty, really, as adult children to carry out this responsibility. Besides, you aren't going to die anytime soon. They will be older and even more mature and responsible when this actually comes to pass. They can figure this out, and we will be here to help."

Rick made a mental note that Ben was the oldest person in the room and then glanced over at Carol. She seemed a little unnerved and was about to ask a question when she was interrupted by Mark.

"I don't know, Ben, they are pretty different ladies. They get along well enough, but some of that may be because they don't interact a lot. This could be a real strain. We have a lot of assets we want them to preserve for our grandchildren, you know, as a legacy," he said.

Rick suggested they could discuss the role a trustee plays and how to choose a trustee purposefully, to take into account the needs of specific beneficiaries. Carol seemed interested as Rick said "purposefully," but Mark wasn't sure because it sounded pricey. He asked Ben if a lengthy trusteeship was expensive and worthwhile.

"Well, you could use a corporate trustee or other professional trustee. They all charge about the same. It's a formula. You should choose a trustee who brings a technical skill set and balanced temperament to the job. Somebody who is logical and a good left-brain decision-maker. It is a job too, it's hard work, and they should be paid. We can set that in the will so it's not too high. If you want that, I can add that to the will," added Ben.

Carol still wasn't sure and asked Rick, "You mentioned a very specific word that caught my attention, you said 'purposeful.' What did you mean by a purposeful trustee choice?"

"Well, a trust is a relationship at its core. The trustee, or executor, has a relationship with the beneficiaries. A relationship established and described in the will. It's a job in one way, I would agree. However, I feel it is much more than that and can be planned for in that manner. It's—"

Rick was interrupted by Mark, who said, "My dad was the executor for his parents and it was pretty easy. There really wasn't much to do. My thinking is we keep it simple for the girls and just use them as executors together. Maybe with you as a tiebreaker, Ben? Or some other lawyer from your firm?" asked Mark.

"Sure. An independent tiebreaker is a great idea and it makes things efficient to wrap up the estate. We often do that for clients," said Ben.

After another half hour of similar banter, Liz mercifully interjected, "Well, this has been a very productive meeting. Mark, Carol, you have some great ideas to work with to update your wills with Ben. I really appreciated being in this conversation so I could understand what was being considered. It helps me serve you better. And Rick, thanks for offering some insights from your experience. Ben, Rick will forward you some of his thoughts and suggestions. When you have the new wills executed, may I have copies for my records?"

Ben asked Mark and Carol if that was acceptable and they agreed. Everyone shared goodbyes and they went to the elevator. As the doors closed, Rick observed Carol glancing at his business card and back up to Rick with an unsettled look on her face. He thanked Liz for the interaction and Ben for being so generous with his time in attending the meeting. As he waited for the elevator, he reflected on Carol's apparent discomfort. He was also unhappy with the path the conversation had taken. He didn't like the feeling.

● ● ●

Later, sitting in his office looking out at yet another evening rainstorm, Rick recognized that the meeting with the Gumbles was all too typical. He had collected a lot of data but didn't really sense that he knew the goals these clients were trying to achieve. He had enough facts to make good technical suggestions but wasn't sure the fuller context was complete. He was surprised to experience a profound desire to never again allow a future meeting to take that trajectory.

At that moment, Rick's friend Auston walked by the office and tapped on the door.

"Why the long face, Rick?" he asked.

Rick gestured to the window and said, "For starters, the weather is grim."

"It's been like that all summer. Tough meeting? I saw you in the boardroom with Liz, a couple of clients and their lawyer."

"Auston, it was a meeting that was so predictable and standard. Everybody talked *at* the clients and didn't let *them* speak *to* us. The questions weren't curious and open-ended, they were confirming solutions already decided. It was—" he was cut off by Auston.

"Frustrating?" Auston asked. "I read a really good book called *Thinking, Fast and Slow*. It's filled with a ton of information about human decision-making behavior, but one interesting thing I recall was that most people—and experts are not immune—only ask questions that tend to confirm their pre-existing conclusions. They don't ask questions that challenge their plan. It leads to all kinds of decision-making problems."

"We need to help people improve their decision-making processes. They need a strategic process to consider risks and threats. They should also assess opportunities and strengths. That kind of SWOT analysis can be done for all kinds of things, in business or in personal finances. And estate planning is no less an opportunity. It could be strategic," thought Rick aloud.

"It's not the norm. Most people just want to keep it cheap and efficient," said Auston.

"Why do you suppose that is? I mean, you're a financial planner—why is it treated like an afterthought, an event rather than a process? Why is strategy not a consideration?" Rick asked.

Auston sat down and thought for a second. He stared at the falling rain and said slowly, "The clients see no value. There is no value to them. It's like buying a flat-screen television. They can go anywhere and get the same thing, so why pay additional dollars? It's a commodity."

Rick stared at Auston and realized the harsh truth in his observation: When a service is reduced to a commodity, the provider is really just an order-taker focused on getting things done. They hadn't been taking the time to plumb deeper for opportunities to add real value or process for their clients. They were just scrolling through checklists.

"I tend to agree. I'm curious, though: when you say value, what do you mean by that?" Rick asked.

"Well, something that differentiates, beyond just a document that works. The outcome of a commoditized estate-planning process is a simple will, powers of attorney, maybe a little tax planning—all the things you'd expect. However, I would describe value-added service in this area as providing a process to follow, a multidisciplinary network of professionals to deal with different issues, a curiosity about understanding and maybe solving those issues, a willingness to check the ego at the door and explore . . . ," Auston trailed off.

"You have given this some thought," said Rick.

Auston explained that he liked the financial plans he developed for clients to be goal-oriented. He wanted to know what the destination was before he plugged the numbers into the algorithm. "People are short-term thinkers and very tax-oriented," he added.

"What do you mean by that?" asked Rick.

"For starters, we, as humans, are naturally loss- and risk-averse. It's part of our evolutionary hardwiring, and a strategic planning process forces us to confront those aversions head-on. In the book I mentioned, the author highlights that the typical person would rather avoid a loss than plan to obtain a similar gain. And by quite a margin," added Auston.

"Huh?" said a bewildered Rick.

Auston decided to give an example he had heard in a podcast. "Consider a room with one thousand people in it," he started. "If I said to everyone on the left half of the audience, so a total of five hundred people . . . ."

Rick laughed, "You don't need to be a financial planner to figure that one out."

"Oh, right," said Auston with a smile before continuing. "The people on the left side are told they must pay one thousand dollars right now. And they do. How do you think they will feel?"

Rick thought for a moment and then responded, "They won't be pleased. They just lost one thousand bucks for no apparent reason. There will be a very large sense of personal and collective loss."

"Right," agreed Auston. "And if I then give the thousand dollars to each of the other five hundred people in the right side of the room, how do you think they will feel?"

"Quite pleased, I would imagine," said Rick.

"Interestingly," said Auston, "the research shows that the people who lost the money will feel much, much worse than the people who received the money will feel better. The two groups, if they were rational actors, should be equally happy as unhappy. But they aren't. It's not a rational response, but it demonstrates how people often react emotionally in a way that is not what you might predict."

"So, in fact, there may not be a concept of common sense. Everything is a personal emotional response and not necessarily rational. One person's response is as valid as another's?" asked Rick.

"That's pretty sweeping," replied Auston. "But it does suggest that we have to ask deeper and more challenging questions to get to the core of the emotion actually driving the behavior."

"What do you mean?" asked Rick.

"Well, I have often observed that anger in a situation is a by-product of fear," said Auston. "The expression of rage, if examined more deeply, is actually a fear of loss of control, love or position."

"Fear and rage are quite different things," said Rick. "Planning for anger and reacting to it is likely very different than acknowledging and managing fear."

"Precisely. And, you can see how fear creeps into planning. Saving a known amount of probate tax with an overly simple plan is much more palatable and real than the notion of potentially establishing certainty and harmony in the family after one's demise. Plus, the deeply held fear of rocking the boat and creating unknown outcomes is a powerful impediment. How can we manage that risk to make better decisions?"

Rick thought about this and made a mental note to consider how to hurdle that challenge. He wanted to discover a way to encourage people to resist the simple solution and invest in the grander vision. He suspected the Convergence conference would provide him with some clues and processes.

"Hmm . . . the combination of short-term thinking and loss aversion renders clients susceptible to overly simplistic planning suggestions," mused Rick aloud.

"It's easier for us because we can get our head around it fast and it provides an answer. There is a sense of accomplishment. The problem is that it avoids the really hard work associated with more purposeful planning," added Auston.

"I think another consideration is that people will stop short on a set of steps unless they see the big picture of the planning. A truly holistic strategic model would really help with that," said Rick.

"What do you mean, Rick?" asked Auston.

"Well, I have observed that clients will often grab the simplest solution that is presented if it seems to deal with a couple of issues presented as stand-alone and vitally important. They tick a box off and they stop there," said Rick.

"It's almost as if they feel that they have a license to stop because they did something," mused Auston.

"Right," continued Rick. "That's a framing issue for advisors. If we frame the client's problem simply and in small nuggets, then that's how they respond to it."

"What we should do is frame the situation larger and create a road map to success," began Auston, raising his voice with excitement.

"Exactly," agreed Rick. "That way, the successes along the path don't impede future progress. They keep going because the larger outcome is the real outcome everyone is working towards."

"A holistic and strategic continuity plan would really help keep people on task," smiled Auston. "As would a coach, Sherpa or advocate along the way. To hold their hands and keep them accountable for actualizing the whole plan and not just the small pieces along the way."

"The processes we use aren't good enough," reflected Rick. "We need something better."

"We need a model to combat the twin problems of short-term planning bias and a willingness to under-frame the true magnitude of the planning experience," Auston summarized.

"You know, the meeting I just finished revealed all of those symptoms. Deeper problems were presenting, but quick and tidy solutions were tossed out and willingly accepted," said Rick.

"Plus, how deep did you really go? Did anyone ask about twenty years from now or even one hundred years from now?" asked Auston.

Rick pondered that question. They hadn't done that at all. "No, not even close," he sighed.

"I should also add that most people don't like dynamic situations filled with contradictions and paradoxes," said Auston.

"Like a family," interjected Rick.

"That's my experience. A ten-thousand-dollar tax saving feels better than the uncertain gain of building or reinforcing a trust relationship," he added.

"Tax savings are tangible," Rick blurted out.

"And a measure of success," said Auston. "Maybe that's why that meeting felt hollow. I don't know what you talked about, but let me guess that the clients were very drawn to saving money, whether in taxes or professional fees."

"Exactly right," said Rick. "And I don't think the wife liked that approach at all. I mentioned purposeful and deliberate planning, and she seemed very intrigued. But then the narrative became about cost and efficiency, and she was silenced."

"I have always thought that people really know the solutions they want. They may not know the structures—you know, trusts, insurance and corporations—but they know what the solution needs to feel like and what it must do and must not do. Our job is to tease their goals and objectives out of them and help them build an appropriate solution," said Auston, checking his watch.

Rick took the cue and said, "I gotta fly too. I think I have a good idea what I need to do now. This will be a tough process, but I think there may be a better way. That is the last time I let a meeting go that way."

"Good luck with that," said Auston as he exited the room. "The system is against you. You are on the road less traveled now. But I'm sure it will be well worth it."

"What do you mean?" asked Rick.

"Look it up, it will make sense . . . talk later," Auston said from down the hall.

Rick googled the poem "The Road Not Taken" on his iPhone and read it on the elevator ride to the parking garage. As he thought about it, the final line of Frost's words was the most resonant: "And that has made all the difference."[1] To Rick, this implied that the change involved in taking the different journey was the reward in itself. He was on to something that was unique and innovative and would alter the way he and his clients engaged with one another.

Rick thought about Auston's comments as he drove home that night. "He's likely right. The system is against me on this and maybe the process can't change. People might think I am an idiot for even suggesting a different path."

As he pulled onto his street, Rick saw his two children playing in the rain on the front lawn. He watched them quietly for a moment. They were why he did everything. He worked to earn money to pay for their dance lessons and give them memories and experiences. He saved wealth for their education that would help them grow into whatever they wanted out of life. He did tax planning as a means to the end of having more money for investment into the family. The focus was the children, not the tax savings. It was no different for anyone else, in that every person should plan holistically for their heirs. Doing anything less was not excusable. Rick was determined to create a model for his clients that he would expect to use upon his own family's wealth.

Just then, a text came in from Dave.

Dave:
Still on the quest?

Rick:
More than ever.

Dave:
Tests await you still, Frodo.

Chapter 2
Purpose

"In the long run, men hit only what they aim at. Therefore, they had better aim at something high."

—Henry David Thoreau

THE DAY HAD FINALLY ARRIVED for Rick to travel to California for the Convergence conference. After a lengthy drive to the airport, he headed to the departure gates, checked his luggage and passed quickly through security. Sitting in the lounge, he sipped on a coffee and people-watched in the terminal.

The whole airport seemed filled with families going this way and that on end-of-summer vacations. Generations from grandparents to grandchildren were schlepping to cottage retreats, beaches and amusement parks to keep up old traditions and make new memories. Rick knew from his own experience how much these moments became the stuff of family legends.

Just then, a father carrying a tray of eight iced cappuccinos stacked in two layers tripped and tossed the entire drink order onto the moving sidewalk. The embarrassment grew worse as his entire family witnessed the mishap in the adjoining gate area. They laughed endlessly as the sticky puddle repeatedly rolled past on the belt every few minutes. A new family legend had been born.

Rick boarded the plane and sat quietly at the window seat he always requested. No one sat beside him for the flight and, after a lengthy snooze and a snack, he used his quiet time to review the fascinating array of planning topics at the conference:

- Wealth and Family Dynamics
- Engaging and Empowering Beneficiaries
- Generational Influences on the Formation of Family Dynamics
- Generational Adaptation to Wealth
- The Power of Giving
- Purposeful Philanthropy

And on and on. The problem for Rick wasn't what to attend, it was what to exclude when choosing his breakout sessions. He marveled at how the seminar topics seemed so different from his typical conference experience. Absent were the usual "Tax Update" and "Tips and Traps on Drafting." This conference was about understanding the client and learning more about himself as an advisor in the process.

• • •

In San Diego, Rick checked into the hotel and stopped by at the conference registration desk to pick up his package of materials. Once he'd unpacked and settled into his room, he headed back downstairs to attend the pre-event dinner out by the swimming pool. There were almost three hundred participants and most were in attendance for the social gathering and opening keynote before Convergence began in earnest the next day.

Rick introduced himself to several people he recognized from the Institute's website and through their weekly podcasts. The other attendees were from all walks of professional life and he was impressed by their candor and passion for holistic planning, the field that had brought them all together at this event.

As he repeatedly discussed his own reasons for attending, he realized he was not alone. The others were present because they also believed or sensed that the technical manner in which they practiced their craft no longer resonated with clients and also lacked meaning for them. They felt that their clients wanted and needed more and were starting to ask for professional wisdom that was deeper and more thoughtful. These advisors were also expressing their own sense of disappointment with the depth of purpose they provided their family clients. Their passion and desire to help their clients had been eroded over time. Rick discovered that many were here on a pilgrimage to rediscover purpose in their own work.

After a long day of travel, Rick decided to pack it in early. He grabbed a scotch at the bar and headed into the hotel lobby towards the bank of elevators. As the doors closed, he saw a pair of hands push in and keep the doors from shutting. The woman attached to the hands let out a loud yelp. Startled, Rick repeatedly pressed the door-open button so the woman wouldn't lose her fingers. The doors re-opened and the woman came aboard the elevator. He noticed she also had a Convergence name lanyard.

"Thanks. I don't know why I always do that," the woman said, smiling as she rubbed her hands together. "It's been a long travel day and I'm pretty exhausted." Then, pointing at the scotch in Rick's hand, she said, "You have the right idea."

He tipped his drink in agreement and asked what floor she needed.

"Top floor, please. Up to the lounge," she said.

"You've been here before," said Rick. "I didn't even know there was a lounge up there."

"Well, come on up and see. Our company is hosting an event for clients and some conference attendees. The view is pretty spectacular. I can introduce you to some people. I'm Angela," she said, thrusting out her recently saved hand to shake.

They exchanged some chatter and Rick decided he might as well see who was at the reception before calling it a night.

The doors opened onto the rooftop lounge area which did, indeed, provide a spectacular view of San Diego. Angela pointed out some landmarks and places to visit if he had some extra time.

"So your company is here in San Diego?" Rick asked.

"We run a multi-family office and have offices across the country. I live here but was travelling from a client's place in Miami. Del Mar is home for me," Angela added.

"Is this your first time at this conference?" asked Rick.

"Oh, not at all. We have been a major sponsor of this event for the last several years. It's my fifth conference. It's the highlight of the continuing education year for me," she said.

"I'm sorry I didn't notice your company is a sponsor," he apologized sheepishly. "I'm a little pooched from the flights as well as the change in the time zone."

She laughed, nodded at the scotch he was holding and said, "So many factors. No problem. You will see our banners around the event pavilions. I introduce several of the speakers."

"What brought you to this conference as a sponsor?" he asked.

"Well, we're building a unique wealth management experience for our clients based on holistic planning. We don't just manage their financial wealth, we help them visualize and then act upon the true potential of their family's total wealth. We are about four years into this and it has been amazingly well-received. This conference is aligned with the core principles of our firm's wealth management approach. Frankly, many of the thought leaders that speak here become part of the education modules we create for our family enterprise clients. That's why we sponsor," she smiled. "What brings you here?"

Rick explained his experience with Claire and the Gumbles and the general sense of discouragement he had with his work.

"You're on a journey," she said. "I was too. I was doing financial plans and was focused on upselling product. That was fine and appropriate, but I asked myself, 'Is this the reason I got into this?' I actually had an experience not unlike your own," she stated.

Angela went on to share her story and, indeed, it was similar to Rick's experience with his client Claire.

"I feel like this conference will be transformative for me," he said.

She nodded and continued, "I learn something new every year. Just keep an open mind. I went back to the office after the first conference and started changing all of my protocols with clients. It has dramatically improved how we compete in the market."

"Are the clients asking for this level of depth and integration? I mean, you're a few years in now, does it work?" Rick asked.

"It has been the best move we ever made," Angela replied. "I love my work again, my colleagues are energized and the clients are demanding our model. It's our competitive advantage. Our market competitors are struggling to catch up and we have acquired many of their best clients. It has been transformative in so many ways," she effused. "And you know what?"

"What's that?" asked Rick.

"I almost didn't do it. I almost didn't attend and we almost stopped in our tracks during the implementation," she said wistfully.

"Too much change at once?" asked Rick.

"That's a great insight. Exactly, it was too much change for us. We had no real strategy. A desire to change is not a strategy. We needed to circle back and develop our own sense of purpose and identify our core values and goals. Once we did that, we were able to start down the path of assisting our clients in doing the same things," she added.

"Physician, heal thyself," smiled Rick.

"It made a difference," she continued. "We also did a lot of re-search on decision-making models, wealth management as a system of thought and creating process. As advisors, we had a lot to learn from outside the narrow silos of our expertise. That said, after the first few hiccups it really blasted off and now, well, the rest as they say is history."

"What's your role now?" asked Rick.

"I'm the education director for all of our households. We have a comprehensive learning model we use with our families on subjects ranging from next generation preparedness for wealth to business succession. I couldn't believe the success. Which was part of what almost killed our model before it was born," she trailed off.

"Change is difficult," mused Rick. "As humans, we aren't very good at imagining how great a change can be for us, so we don't change. It feels easier to accept what we have always done as the way things will always be."

"Precisely. What a mistake that would have been. We would still be in the old world of planning and telling people what we want them to do," Angela finished as Rick suppressed a small yawn.

Not noticing that he was out of social gas, Angela made a few introductions to her partners and two speakers. By this time Rick was getting truly dopey and decided to say goodnight. They agreed to touch base the next day and share notes on their experiences.

In the elevator down to his room, Rick texted his wife and said good night. The adventure was set to begin.

• • •

When the sessions began the following day, every speaker impressed Rick with a mind-boggling array of potential conversations and solutions available to clients, all fundamentally different from the same old routine advisor-client engagement. He quickly appreciated that he was one of the few lawyers in attendance. He pondered that reality with some sadness as a keynote speaker lamented the negative effects of the billable hour on the estate-planning element of the legal profession.

For most lawyers, will planning had become a commodity—a quick-and-dirty boilerplate process that checked off a to-do list for clients and was a loss-leader to bring in other business for the firm. Yet, for clients it was centrally important to their lives. Making their will was a milestone in their life and a key part of creating a legacy for their family. It was a meaningful document that offered an opportunity to share their vision, gratitude and pride. Or at least it should be. Rick now realized more acutely than ever that estate planning, including creating a will, establishing a family trust or succession planning for a family business, was a process and not an event. To be successful, wealth-transition planning required attention to goal development, effective communication and authentic process.

He pondered this realization after attending a presentation on the psychology of money between generations. He started to frantically make notes as ideas and insights burst forth into his mind. Through the hours of the program, one question that had seemed rather innocuous at first took on more resonance for Rick as he reflected more deeply after each speaker. He had written down the question: Estate Planning versus Wealth-Continuity Planning?

After each speaker, he jotted thoughts and takeaways in his journal. An answer to his question was beginning to take shape. Later that day, exhausted from a full conference experience, he relaxed by the pool with a neat scotch.

"Hey, I didn't see you much today, Rick. How are you?" It was Angela, whom he had met the first evening.

"I'm pooped. That was a lot of varied content for my old brain," he smiled.

She sat at the end of his lounge chair and asked him, "Any epiphanies today? Something that will be a game changer for your world view?"

"More of a question, really. Something I think marks the real change that is going on," said Rick.

"Fire away," laughed Angela. "What's the question?"

"Is what we do best described as estate planning or wealth-continuity planning?" he said.

Angela paused for a moment to reflect on the question. "What's your sense so far?" she asked.

"Good deflection," he smiled. "Okay, I have always called it estate planning. It's incremental tactics, managing money and shepherding financial assets towards a single event."

"Typically death," added Angela. "It ends there in most cases."

"Right. And that's a problem as well. But the more insightful aspect I am realizing is that the beginning is not an event either. It's a process without a beginning and an end. It's a story and a responsibility that may never end," he stopped. "Does that sound stupid?"

She laughed and said, "Not at all. You are experiencing the difference now. It's a continuous process of planting, growing and harvesting. The real question becomes, what really is the wealth of a family and how should you deploy the financial assets to grow that wealth?"

"Those are much different questions than asking what your assets are and who gets them," Rick laughed. "So continuity planning is a much better description," he added.

"The old way is simple estate planning. It's geared towards solving temporal problems and not generating continuous opportunity. It is tactical rather than strategic. What you will learn as you experience more of this purposeful approach is that family wealth is destroyed between generations by the old way of doing things. A continuity-based model avoids the entropy effect of intergenerational wealth transition. That was a hurdle when we got started," said Angela.

"I assume that's because it required you as a group to accept that what you had always done wasn't the best way and that there was much to learn?" said Rick.

"For sure," agreed Angela. "Wisdom only comes from understanding how little you actually know."

"But clients come to us for answers. It's not easy to say you don't know the answer," thought Rick aloud.

"That is true, and it means a process is required to manage the expectations of the client. We must help them to ask better questions and demand broader responses from their advisors and from themselves. Haven't you always felt that your clients knew the solutions to their problems before they met with you?" she asked.

Rick thought about the question and answered, "You know, it's true. They know what has to happen and what can't happen. They just don't know the tactics like trusts, corporations, wills . . . you know . . . to put it into effect."

"Well, they aren't lawyers and accountants," laughed Angela.

"Although the world could use more of each," added Rick with a wry smile.

They both laughed at the utter lunacy of that statement.

"I think what many families really need is some helping hands to become advocates for their own planning. They don't need to be told what to do, they want to create the plan themselves and let the subject matter architects build the structure," said Rick.

"And I think that goes to the nub of your initial question," said Angela. "Is it estate planning or wealth-continuity planning? Families with a vision for their family wealth create continuity plans. People who don't care beyond keeping it transactional, simple and efficient do estate planning."

"It's an important distinction. You can call it what you want, but the difference is in the details of the process," said Angela as she checked her watch. "Whoops, it's late. I have to hit the hay. See you tomorrow and we can chat again."

Angela and Rick said their goodnights to one another and then Rick did a final loop around the pool area to stretch his legs. As he walked he decided that continuity planning would be his preferred moniker for his future approach to intergenerational wealth planning. The estate is what gets processed when you die. Estate planning means having a will, having a power of attorney, having life insurance to pay taxes or achieve some other tactical need. Continuity planning means having a long-term vision and strategic plan for the wealth of the family. Back in his room, he grabbed his journal and wrote down all the ideas before he fell asleep.

• • •

The next morning, Rick attended the keynote in the main conference theatre. The day's keynote speaker, Tom Hill, delivered a thoughtful family business story describing how poor planning and complicated family dynamics had mixed to destroy his family's second-generation agriculture business.

Tom's parents, Reginald and Edna, owned a farm operation that was ironically named Blissful Acres. His parents were in their seventies when the story began, and Tom described how he, his brother and sister were friendly enough but not that close. He had moved off the farm after going to journalism school and never returned except for family events. His brother, Cal, remained on the farm his whole life, working it with his parents. Their sister, Trina, had struggled both financially and with relationships in her life. She had lived on the farm in a small cottage behind the main house after her second divorce.

Reginald had been to his lawyer on two occasions to discuss the succession of Blissful Acres. He had variously described his general desire to pass the farm operation to Cal to reflect his son's efforts over the years. Cal had always understood he would get the farm upon his parents' death. Reginald had also talked to his bookkeeper and to his accountant on many occasions about his desire to get the farm to Cal. Despite many such conversations and meetings, nothing was ever done. These meetings and conversations had taken place over many years until the year Reginald turned eighty and received a cancer diagnosis. It was then that things really went downhill in a hurry.

Shortly after Reginald's diagnosis, Edna began a rapid mental deterioration from her dementia. Edna was three years older than her husband and was soon legally incompetent. She had done a will that left everything to her three children in equal shares. With Edna legally constrained by her illness, the will document could not be amended. However, Reginald solely owned most of the farm operation. He knew that, with Edna incapable and his own cancer diagnosis, time was running out to give effect to his farm transition plan. He visited his pastor and a friend who was retired from law on several occasions and expressed a desire to get the farm to Cal.

And yet, through it all, nothing was accomplished to advance his desire to transfer the farm. For various reasons that were not explored by his advisors, Reginald never discussed the plan with the other children. One Sunday evening he took a turn for the worse and he died the next morning.

Reginald's will exactly mirrored Edna's. His entire estate went to his legally incompetent spouse when he passed away. She died two years later and the estate was divided three equal ways. In between, Cal sued his father's estate and then his mother's when she passed away. Cal and Trina never got along before their parents died and the family fractured badly from the litigation. Trina desperately needed the inheritance, and the farm was the only real asset. It was a total disaster.

Rick listened intently as Tom detailed the basic facts, the timeline and the ultimate outcome of his family's despair. Tom then asked the audience to think about what had *really* caused the wealth to dissipate. Audience members volunteered a variety of legal and tax pitfalls that had been described. There were so many suggestions made that the time ran out and conference-goers had to move on to their next sessions.

Rick thought about Tom's session and the question he posed at the end as he walked to a session on "Coping with Sudden Wealth." He wasn't sure the answers proffered were the real reason for the failure and litigation. He resolved to find Tom at lunch and suggest another reason.

• • •

At the completion of the morning sessions, Rick quickly grabbed some salad and coffee for lunch. He looked around the seating areas and finally spotted Tom texting on his phone in the resort lounge. Rick began to approach the lounge to make an introduction, when he felt a gentle tap on his shoulder. Looking back, he saw it was Angela.

"Hey, how was your morning, Rick?" she asked as they gave a quick hug.

"It was great. I enjoyed all the sessions. How was yours?" he asked.

"I really liked the keynote. We work with a lot of family businesses and their families, and that story was eerily familiar," she said.

"I was just going to say hello to Tom there in the lounge. I wanted to run something by him. Come with me?" asked Rick.

Angela agreed, and they headed down to the lounge and introduced themselves to Tom Hill. He was very gracious and asked them to join him for coffee.

"What did you think of my presentation?" Tom asked.

Angela explained her experiences with similar circumstances and how it saddened her to see these outcomes happen. "The families often fracture and never connect again. The cost is very high. Have you been able to bridge the divide and make peace with your siblings?" she asked Tom.

"Not really," he told her. "I talk to Trina and her children. But neither of us has much to do with Cal. After he sued the estate a lot of harsh words were said. Words that are difficult to unsay. We are trying, though, and time will tell. The farm had to be sold and Cal needed to find a job. He went to work for another farmer and really seemed to lose his spark in life. It was sad for him. He lost his spouse and his life's work. I hope I didn't make him out as a villain, he was a victim too."

"I thought about the causes, Tom," said Rick.

"And?" Tom asked.

"Well, the legal issues people suggested around the will and the incompetency of your mother are all accurate, but they seem to miss the real point . . . they avoid the real nub that caused the problem," started Rick.

"I had thought maybe your parents were to blame for not getting anything done," interjected Angela. "But that seemed inaccurate as well."

Rick nodded and continued, "No, I agree. That's not it either. I think the real cause was that nobody grabbed the situation by the horns and helped unstick your father, in particular, from his quandary. He knew he had to do something and he couldn't get there to actually do it. He needed a coach, a mentor or a guide to get him through that blockage, whatever it was."

Tom smiled and said, "That's my feeling as well. He needed a 'champion,' someone to really take time and get to the core of the problem. To ask hard and fierce questions and challenge the answers. My dad needed someone to understand—"

"His perspective," interjected Angela. "He needed someone to understand how he saw the situation and to explore whether it was appropriate or fair. He may have needed permission to speak candidly about a situation he was deeply worried would destroy the balance of the family."

"His opinion may have differed from your mother's as well," added Rick. "You may have no idea now."

Tom nodded and confirmed he had no idea at all. They hadn't talked much and communication was poor. To this very day he was unsure what really prevented his father from putting something concrete in place.

"It's curious that you should say 'concrete,'" added Rick. "I have found that making a plan permanent and decided is often a blockage in itself. Many shareholder agreements and wills aren't signed because the very act of putting your name to ink has a profound sense of solemnity and permanence. If they won't sign it, they don't like it."

Just then, the lobby music quieted and the venue lights flickered signaling the end of the lunch period. Conference attendees began heading to their breakout sessions for the afternoon. Rick stood and shook Tom's hand. It appeared they were heading towards the same conference area while Angela said her thanks and started off in a different direction.

"You know, Tom," started Rick as they walked. "It seems to me that your parents needed someone to hold them accountable for achieving their planning goals. To make sure they were taking steps forward and helping them remove obstacles."

"Yes," said Tom. "And they would have benefited from a process or a peer group to guide their decision-making. You know, something that allowed them to have their say, garner opinions from others and have a process to assess the next steps needed on their path when they settled on a goal. They were in over their heads."

The two men shook hands again as Tom veered to another room for a presentation. Rick sat down and made notes in his journal about his conversation with Tom. His parents needed a process. As Rick listened to the speaker on the subject of "Building a Trustworthy and Effective Beneficiary," an idea for a process came into his mind. It started small at first, but soon the basic framework was written down.

• • •

As the final session ended, Rick decided to head to the pool area and grab a drink. He looked around for some other conference delegates and noticed one at a table near the tiki bar. He had briefly met Francisco in the final session. Fran was also a lawyer but, in a career pivot, had recently become a speaker after writing several successful books on family business succession planning.

"Mind if I join you, Francisco?" asked Rick.

"Not at all. Please, call me Fran," he said as they shook hands.

"That was a very curious day," said Rick.

"Curious?" inquired Fran.

"I have to confess, I had modest expectations for the conference. I really wasn't sure what to expect but decided to push the envelope a little and take a chance," said Rick.

Fran started, "I had the same reservations last year when I attended. It looked . . ."

"Fluffy?" interrupted Rick.

Fran continued. "Yes, sort of. I was so used to the usual technical topics. I am sure you know what I mean. I love that stuff too, but these broader concepts are considerably more holistic. They really stretch the mind and help you get to the core of the client's planning concerns."

"I now realize how prescriptive our profession is in the wealth-continuity and estate-planning field," said Rick.

"What do you mean?" asked Fran.

"Well, I spend all my time *telling* clients what they need instead of trying to determine what they really want," said Rick. "I often go straight to the solution in my head, based on the rules of play for my profession. What I have heard from the speakers so far is that I should let the clients search out their own expression of the solution. Then, as a technical expert, I can build it for them. One speaker suggested that most clients know the answers to their own questions, they just don't know how to build the structure. It's funny," Rick continued, "I was discussing the very same thing with a colleague a week or so ago. As I told him then, I feel like the suggestions I make are determined before I even really understand the client—I have the answer before I really understand the question. But there isn't one set of rules that perfectly applies to every family. Each family is unique. Yet, we bolt them into one-size-fits-all structures. It's no wonder there is so much litigation; none of the solutions authentically fit the real needs of the family."

"That kind of formulaic planning sets the whole exercise on a course for failure," said Fran. "We stop thinking outside the box and play by the rules we know. It's important to go beyond our professional silo and create a broader conversation. It's like that saying by Abraham Maslow. I think it goes something like, 'If the only tool in your toolkit is a hammer, after a while, all the problems you face start to look like nails.'" He laughed.

"Well, yes," said Rick. "Technical expertise is necessary, but it can sometimes come at a cost to the family if there isn't sufficient breadth of skill or an innovative mindset. Or at least the ability to identify an external planning need and seek it out first before locking onto a technical structure. It must be frustrating for clients. They are seeking wisdom but getting the tyranny of technical prowess instead."

"True," agreed Fran. "And it's often hard to find those two mindsets together in the same person. Part of that is a function of the complexity of modern planning; it's very hard to stay on top of everything. I think we need a model or series of questions we can ask to conduct a better discovery process. You know, to really get to the root of the matter . . . to effectively dig in and establish what makes this person tick," he finished.

"Will people pay for that?" asked Rick.

"Clients will always pay for value," said Fran. "Especially these days, with so much baseline information available for free on the Internet. Think about it: technology is replacing almost any procedure based on a checklist. Using a checklist? There will be an app for that. You better have some compelling value to add beyond technical skill to survive in that kind of world."

Rick gave his words some thought and agreed that clients do understand the investment required to obtain insight and the inherent value of a more strategic approach. He decided to change the subject slightly and asked Fran, "Why are you here? What made you move to this type of planning model?"

"Good question," he responded. "About five years ago, a friend passed away rather suddenly at sixty. He was the happiest person I knew. He had a boundless joy about his life. People were so sad at his death, but his family seemed at peace. He had been planning for that moment his entire adult life, long before he ever became ill. When he died, it was a seamless transition," added Fran.

"He was planning for his death his whole life?" asked Rick.

"In a way, yes, he did. He was very communicative and shared his goals and love for his daughters every day. As a family, they talked openly about difficult issues and he sought their opinions. They fought, like every family. They had sad times and happy times. They were successful financially. The children were each differently skilled. It was a typical situation," said Fran.

"So the wealth went to the wife?" asked Rick.

"Not all of it. A fund was created for the education and financial stability of the family from one generation to the next. They used life insurance to create what they called their 'opportunity fund.' The idea was that it was possible to attain financial freedom in many ways but that education was the key in their family," clarified Fran.

"Like college or university?" queried Rick.

"In part, but what they really wanted to do was make sure that the children had a healthy relationship with wealth. To not be afflicted with *affluenza*," added Fran.

Rick laughed. He had heard that term before and had seen it in his professional life. It described the malaise of isolation and indolence often caused by receiving substantial unearned wealth. "I actually encountered a situation where a fifty-year-old son lived in the basement of his mother's house watching TV and playing video games for the sole purpose of exerting as little energy as possible before the financial windfall that would occur upon his mother's eventual death. He died of diabetes-related conditions before his mother," he added.

"Well, they do say that sitting in chairs for too long is the new smoking," Fran chuckled. "Sadly, we all have stories like that, although not always with the ironic twist. A dysfunctional relationship with money is toxic and spreads its poison far and wide. The child waiting on the inheritance fails to learn how to manage money, and life in general, because they never needed to develop those skills. Pretty soon after they get the windfall, they lose it. That's what my friend successfully avoided. He decided to use his financial wealth to invest into the full abundant potential of his family members."

Thinking about Fran's words, Rick added, "Or they lose friends, marriages, families, jobs . . . even motivation and purpose. They forfeit the spice of life, the snap in their celery."

"In my friend's case," explained Fran, "the trustees were selected with great care and introduced to the beneficiaries while the parents were still alive to develop an ongoing and long-lasting relationship with the whole family. It was a trial run in some ways, to test the commitment and potential of the trustee–beneficiary relationship," said Fran.

"His wife survived, so that wasn't needed, I suppose," said Rick.

"True," agreed Fran. "But she was so committed to their vision that she maintained the relationships they had introduced to their children and the whole process will continue at her eventual death. Every year, they all meet for a dinner and get caught up. The trustees are a close family friend and his wife, and they participated with the children in classes on financial management delivered by the wife's investment advisor."

"Wow, they are also modelling some fantastic engagement to their children. So, she stayed with the same advisor after her husband died?" asked Rick.

"Against the odds, yes. And the reason was that the advisor was very progressive and had a long-term approach to his relationships, not only with his clients but also with their families. He was their *family* advisor. He refrained from calling himself a 'trusted advisor' or 'most trusted advisor,'" added Fran.

"That is pure cheese," laughed Rick. "Every advisor is trusted. That's why clients keep them as advisors."

Fran chuckled in agreement and continued. "I suppose there is some room for the moniker 'most trusted advisor.' In my experience, that is typically someone whose input is perceived to be so objective and filled with breadth that they transcend any professional role they fill. They become family. In fact, in this case the investment advisor did the eulogy at his client's funeral."

"Really? Were they old friends?" asked Rick.

"Nope. They met professionally. It was simply an authentic and multi-layered interaction," said Fran.

"That is amazing, and what a blessing for the family," added Rick.

"It made the whole transition easier and gave it great purpose," said Fran. "It wasn't just a transition of money, it was also a transition of wisdom, process and knowledge. It was a relationship that altered through transformation but did not end. It was about the beneficiaries and not the tax man."

"That struck you as good planning?" asked Rick.

"I really had to think about it because it was so unusual," replied Fran. "I asked myself, 'Why do we plan?' The answer at first was to reduce tax and get the money to the beneficiaries. But I realized my friend didn't see it that way. His family took time to build a relationship with the wealth so that they were ready for it when it was received. It was not a burden or a curse but a source of growth; not only would the plan they developed sustain and protect their wealth upon their death, but it also worked to generate new wealth and abundance for future generations in the family. The full extent of the family's wealth—not only the financial capital, but also their shared values and priorities—was used for investment into the next generation. Really, he was preparing his family for the financial wealth rather than preparing the financial wealth to pass to the heirs."

Rick seemed lost in thought as he pondered that concept.

"That's the complete opposite of what is usually done," Fran added. "Typically, planners worry about probate, estate tax, privacy and efficiency in the estate planning first . . . and then they consider the readiness, needs and goals of the heirs almost as an afterthought, if at all."

Rick recalled the image of his children playing in the rain on the front lawn. This was all starting to make sense. "He planned to enhance the lives of his family," he said to Fran. "That is a different mindset. So many people plan only if they perceive risk or weakness in their heirs. But that way of thinking is negative in nature."

"And sometimes that is needed," said Fran. "The problem is that where no risk or weakness is perceived, the planning tends to stop. Or, people aren't honest with themselves about what is likely to happen in the future. I am reminded of a television commercial where a large crowd is asked to tabulate the good things and bad things that happened in the past year," Fran continued. "In general, the good and bad are about equal. Life is like that. Then they are asked to predict whether good things or bad things will happen in the year ahead. Overwhelmingly, they predict good things. Against their own recently reported experience, they are overly optimistic about the future,"

"When I ask clients if they are comfortable with their in-laws and how capable their children are with money, the answers are overwhelmingly positive and optimistic," said Rick.

Fran interjected. "Despite the high incidence of divorce, unexpected career changes, stress events, disease and economic dislocation."

"People are optimistic . . . that seems like a good thing," said Rick.

"It's also why some people accept it when they are told that if a beneficiary can't handle money by age thirty-five or some other age, they will never learn how to, and so people think, well, you can't rule from the grave, so just give it to them—they'll manage and, who cares if they blow it?" added Fran with a tinge of anger.

Rick shuddered and said, "I hear that all the time. I have recently tried to challenge people on that way of thinking so I can really understand their frame of reference," stated Rick.

"How do they respond?" asked Fran.

"The answers usually suggest they have an understanding of intergenerational wealth planning, or estate planning, as a single event rather than as a lengthy and effort-demanding process," said Rick.

"What do you mean?" asked Fran.

"Well, for example, they will say things like, 'It's their money, it's a gift to them; I don't want to attach strings, I want them to enjoy it as they wish,' you know, things like that," explained Rick.

"That reflects a lack of knowledge about the true potential of financial wealth," added Fran.

"Yes," agreed Rick. "No strings means they aren't ruling from the grave. But we aren't talking about an event that starts a process when a person dies. We are talking about a lifelong purposeful process of which death is simply an inflection point for the wealth. In fact, death is the new beginning of the next phase of the strategic plan. It's a seamless tapestry."

Fran agreed with the seamless tapestry image and added, "I think some people believe that 'parenting' beyond the grave is a bad thing. Certainly, it's important to allow and encourage our heirs to be independent and successful in their own right. There is indeed a time to parent and a time to let go. That may be at the core of the statement . . . they equate it with unending parenting beyond the grave."

"Or they think it reflects a lack of trust . . . or worse," said Rick.

"Worse?" asked Fran.

"Some people are malevolent in their will plans," explained Rick. "I once read a plan where an older chap had married a younger woman after his first wife died. His new wife was only slightly older than his eldest daughter. For reasons he never did reveal, his spouse and daughter didn't get along. So he created a trust for some financial wealth that would benefit the wife with income during her lifetime and the remaining capital would pass on her death to his daughter."

Fran gasped a little and then started chuckling, "But they are the same age; the daughter will probably never see it."

"It gets worse," said Rick. "The daughter is the trustee."

"They should both avoid steep stairwells for the rest of their lives," laughed Fran. "Gosh, that was almost deliberate cruelty. Was he trying to send a message?"

"He wouldn't tell me," said Rick. "He only ever just smiled. I reminded him that, unless they could mend their fences, they would be in mortal combat over that gift for the rest of their lives. But, again, he just smiled. It bothered me a little at the time. That's the stuff people hear about in the coffee shops. I don't accept that it shouldn't be done, I just think we need to show a better way."

"That's how my friend felt and it's why I am here this week. There is a better way and it is worth trying," said Fran.

"To avoid the 'shirtsleeves to shirtsleeves' phenomenon?" asked Rick.

"Yes," Fran answered. "I believe a more strategic continuity-planning process will work to sustain wealth for more than three generations. Not only that, but also to ensure that when I ask 'Why do I plan?' I understand the answer myself. Personally, I plan for my children. I want them to succeed and I want it to be on their terms. I don't want to rule from the grave; instead I want to use my lifetime to create conversations, traditions and governance around the total-ity of my family's wealth so that every generation in my family can develop into careful and effective stewards of the family legacy," finished Fran, looking at his watch.

Rick thought about the conversation and then added, "You view the wealth-continuity planning process as one of creation and re-creation, not an act of destruction."

As he got up to leave, Fran looked at Rick thoughtfully and said, "I never thought of it that way. Yes, to avoid the destructive effect of entropy on wealth that moves between generations, it behooves us as planners, and our clients, to be innovative and generative in our planning. Moreover, this highlights that it is a process, not a singular act or event. I also really like the word 'continuity' because it highlights the process component. I hear you using it too. Good for you."

They said good evening and Rick walked towards the tented dining area where a conference dinner was being served. He sat with a large group of financial planners and investment advisors and enjoyed their familiar conversations. He skipped dessert and went back to the pool area to reflect on the day's learnings.

It was a warm California evening and the torches around the pool reminded Rick of his favorite vacation spot, Hawaii. He reclined on a lounge chair and as he looked up to a clear, starry sky, he pondered that idea again—the wealth-continuity planning process as a process of creation rather than orderly destruction. It is about building an intergenerational family legacy rather than simply splitting the family wealth up among beneficiaries. It is a process and not an event. He realized this may be the "eureka" moment he was seeking in order to adjust the course of his planning narrative.

He also reflected upon his favorite session of the day, presented by Zara Winters. Rick was immediately taken by the bold title of the presentation, "Estate Planning for the 21st Century." It suggested, by implication, that all other planning was ineffective and out of touch with modern realities. Zara's message was simple: the world has changed and the old ways of viewing intergenerational wealth are actually destructive to family dynamics and to the wealth of clients in the twenty-first century. As she finished, the applause had been slow at first but then became very loud and appreciative. Something new was spoken that afternoon and the thoughtful in the crowd felt it resonate.

As Rick continued to reflect on that presentation, he happened to see Zara by the poolside fire. He walked over to introduce himself and congratulated her on her provocative presentation. Rick told her he appreciated that the specific techniques she had covered presumed a high level of client engagement to ensure the concepts would be adopted. In the examples in her presentation, the families had been prepared, the next generations had been readied to receive the wealth (financial and all the other kinds of wealth that go along with it) and the estate planning was implemented as part of a larger strategic approach—innovative intergenerational wealth planning for the entire family.

"That was really insightful," he said.

"It's a little out there . . . did anyone seem offended?" Zara smiled sheepishly.

"It needs to be said," Rick answered. "We live in a new world and people need to understand that planning must take a broader approach. I'm especially impressed that you have a financial-planning background. That's unusual for a lawyer."

"It is a bit," said Zara. "However, in this field it will start to be the norm over the next twenty years. Professionals need to be conversant with clients on many levels. I often collaborate with financial and investment planners, but I really find it enhances the client experience to be comfortable in those areas myself. I used to sheepishly joke that as a financial planner I was a great lawyer, then I decided it wasn't funny anymore."

"I think it's fundamental to modern wealth-continuity planning to be aware of the economy, trends in financial products, taxation and all the usual estate-planning concerns," said Rick. "It's an evolving and difficult area of specialty . . . you cannot be a one-trick pony anymore. The economic argument you raised is fascinating."

"That one is very serendipitous," she said, smiling. "I always believed in purposeful planning, but the events of 2008 and the market meltdown really drove it all home. We don't live in Kansas anymore . . . the world has changed."

"How does that conversation flow with your clients?" he asked.

"Basically, I challenge their notion that you can't rule from the grave. That is a ridiculous statement . . . of course you can. You and I both know that all too well," she said.

Rick agreed. It was very easy to structure someone's affairs to give them control over how their wealth is managed, even after they are deceased. Any good estate lawyer could rhyme off a handful of approaches to achieve that very goal. Trusts, for example, allow clients to dictate the terms of their wealth plan far beyond their own lifetime.

"I have always maintained that the question isn't really whether you can rule from the grave, but whether you should," said Rick.

Zara nodded her agreement and continued. "Even further, I think we need to wrap our heads around an entirely different concept and ask a dramatically new set of questions. Instead of 'rule,' let's say 'influence.' And then recast it another way for clients: 'Why wouldn't you want to influence the future relationship your family has with the wealth you transmitted, to make it a successful one rather than damaging?'"

Rick thought about the question and then said, "Right, that's the true question, and the way you've phrased it is so positive. It removes the negative connotations of 'ruling from the grave.' I just talked about this idea with someone else . . . that estate planning is better conceived and practiced as a process of creation rather than an act of destruction. It is a generative process and not merely a destructive event."

"It is," agreed Zara, "but most advisors and their clients are still concerned with the single act of distributing the estate upon death. They're still preoccupied with what we think of as a destructive act. And that's why wealth is often dissipated by the time the third generation comes along. The answers advisors provide to clients aren't inaccurate, it's just that the wrong questions are being asked in the first place. There is no broader strategic process for the client, an approach that will be ever more vital to acknowledge if these economic conditions persist. Our traditional approach to estate planning actually dissipates and destroys the power of financial wealth," finished Zara, with only a little bit of hyperbole.

"That was no problem when times were good and demographic growth created almost guaranteed economic good times," said Rick. "I mean, recessions occurred, but they were short and followed by a recovery that featured new jobs and rising incomes. However, that's not so true anymore."

"It's not true at all, concurred Zara. "Most recent economic recoveries have been anemic for income growth. Lots of the employment created was temporary or in lower-paying service sectors. Plus, technology is erasing many jobs in the interim. Moreover, as the economists note, we are likely living in an extended era of low growth and lowered interest rates." She went on, saying, "In the old days, you could count on interest rates and income growth to create wealth and capital. That is gone now for the foreseeable future. Your kids can't expect to be able to start a business and get wealthy like you did. They can't expect to be able to take big risks with capital and assume that rebuilding off failure will even be possible. You know how we tell our kids it seems harder for them these days? It is—a lot harder."

"I have heard that half the population believes that they won't be better off than their parents," Rick forlornly added.

"Which is very different from the 1970s generation," pointed out Zara, "when the vast majority of young adults were confident their generation would surpass their parents."

"It seems like a university degree is a prerequisite for employment as a barista," sighed Rick.

"It practically is, Rick. Plus, those jobs don't pay well and these students may emerge from university tens of thousands of dollars in debt. It's a whole different world. Millennials will need to be creative, innovative and entrepreneurial in ways we never imagined," said Zara.

"The jobs won't be there," said Rick, sighing again. "These kids will need access to capital just to keep pace with the bare minimum of educational retraining. They will need to be lifelong learners, but how will they afford that expense?"

"And technology is disrupting the workforce more every year. It's amazing, but scary," said Zara. "Consider your smartphone. Moore's Law predicts that that piece of technology will exceed your brain's computational power within ten years."

"Well, maybe my brain!" said Rick with a laugh. "But isn't that a bit of science fiction? And so what anyway? Vanishing old jobs are always replaced by new ones."

"Maybe," said Zara. "But I think it's safer to consider the scenario that they don't come back. That's the key with planning, Rick. You need to ask, 'Where is everything heading?' Wayne Gretzky is famously quoted as saying something to the effect that success is really about going where the puck will be, not where it is. If you go where something is, it will pass you by the time you get there; you will be chasing. That's bad planning."

Rick nodded his agreement.

"An added risk is that people will fall prey to 'planning fallacy' and simply pay attention to their own historical in-family experiences," continued Zara. "But they really need to look outside the family box and see where the world is headed. The simple estate planning that worked for grandma will not work for you. Future generations will need capital accumulation to drive incomes, wealth and personal economic growth, but capital accumulation may be impossible for many on current wages. They may need the stable pool of income from capital that can be provided from an estate. So planning that preserves and enhances the intergenerational pool of financial wealth will be critical to the success of families going forward."

Rick nodded again. It was all falling into place for him now.

"That's why I prefer to call it intergenerational wealth continuity rather than estate planning," explained Zara. "Estate planning is usually equated with wills and life insurance. They are vital considerations, of course, but creating a model to sustain capital between generations is much, much more than those simple tactics. It is a strategic process rather than a tactical event. It demands a sense of purpose."

"It also demands a growth-oriented, multidisciplinary and collaborative mindset," added Rick.

"The estate-planning paradigm has changed . . . and more change is coming," Zara said as she got up and said good night.

After she left, Rick ordered a Long Island iced tea and enjoyed the remainder of the warm evening. He was heading home the next morning, and so he took a few minutes alone by the pool to reflect on the conference he'd looked forward to for such a long time. He hadn't been disappointed. He now realized that a great deal more was possible in the planning conversation. And, because more was possible, it was apparent to him that not enough was being done. It was time for him to cross the Rubicon from the world as it is to the world as it could be. It was the best professional conference he had ever attended and there was not a single technical presentation in the program.

The next day, rested, fully rejuvenated and intellectually enriched, Rick flew home excited and nervous about the changes that lay ahead as he set a course down this path of purposeful planning. It was a controversial position, to view the estate plan as a creative process rather than merely a point of asset disposition. It would also be unusual to suggest that planning in the traditional mode was the very reason wealth was destroyed between generations. It would be a head scratcher for many clients and advisors to start from this position. However, it was a change whose time had come.

Chapter 3

Building a Better Way
Communication, Values and Mission Statements

"It's not hard to make decisions when you know what
your values are."
 —**Roy Disney**, *former Disney executive, nephew of Walt Disney*

A FEW WEEKS after his return from California, Rick was professionally transformed and had a newly awakened passion for planning. He knew he was in the early stages of a journey that would add powerful resources to his professional toolkit. This would benefit every future client and their families because now every problem would not just look like a nail. He decided to construct a new client engagement model that he could deploy and share with advisors and clients. His new model would be based on an amalgamation of strategic and purposeful concepts to provide continuity of wealth between generations and avoid the wealth entropy of the shirtsleeves-to-shirtsleeves experience.

Rick met clients within a wealth-management setting. After his experience at the Convergence conference, he now appreciated that this context often framed the conversation more squarely on financial assets than was otherwise optimal for purposeful planning. He also knew that wealth-continuity planning conversations of any kind were difficult for clients. Very few people want to exuberantly face their own mortality. As a result, Rick had observed that most people focused on simple tactics as a common way to address the conversation in an accessible manner and get something done. Clients understand a tax-savings tip or risk-management suggestion because they are tangible and consistent with the wealth management context. However, he now believed this approach risked placing the solution before the strategy. He wanted to amend that problem because it was a major contributor to wealth destruction between generations.

In an effort to combat this shortcoming, Rick decided to use this morning at the office to reframe the meaning of wealth management to clients. He wanted a fuller and more generous definition that would broaden the context of the estate–continuity conversation. He did some research and then came up with his own working definition of wealth management:

> *Wealth management is a process. Done holistically, it strives to purposefully and strategically identify, prioritize and satisfy client goals by identifying all sources of family wealth and by introducing financial products and other services to achieve their planning needs in a manner consistent with the client's values and the family's mission.*

Rick liked this definition because it required more of both the advisor and the client. It put the onus on clients to communicate and articulate their wants and needs; and on the advisor to be curious and uncover these goals and priorities, and to see to their client's satisfaction. In addition, it suggested that part of the advisor's role is coordinating a team of subject-matter experts, which demands some knowledge of those topics and an extensive network of professional connections to share with the client. Most importantly, it conveyed that wealth management is a positive and strategic process designed to create, sustain and steward all sources of family wealth. It was the process that was missing from Tom Hill's family story in San Diego. It was the process Rick was building to change his world.

"That definition is a good starting point for a client discussion," he thought to himself. "I can explore my clients' understanding of the idea and then compare where they are hoping to go with where they are today. Managing the gap between the two locations is the terrain of effective strategy and planning."

Rick's desired outcome was to build a truly strategic approach to the family wealth-continuity experience. As a test, he had been successfully integrating modular components of his evolving continuity-planning model into his various client interactions since his return from California. He was now ready to assemble a comprehensive model for all clients.

"The last few weeks of testing elements of my new model have been interesting," he mused. "Many of the people had no idea what I was talking about when I mentioned a strategic approach to wealth-continuity planning. They didn't really appreciate what is meant by strategy. They most often equated it with tactics." Rick resolved to build a model that would explain the elements of successful strategy, wealth management and wealth-continuity planning.

• • •

As 11 a.m. rolled by, Rick desperately needed to clear the fog in his brain. He wandered out of the office and headed for a walk around the neighborhood. It was a beautiful morning and the early September sun was cascading through the tops of the silver maple trees above the eastern horizon.

Rick circled the city's central public park once and then cut diagonally across the park to enter into Wendel's Roastery, a local coffee shop. He went to the counter and ordered a dark-roast Kona coffee and a breakfast sandwich.

"Thanks, Amy," he told the girl behind the counter. "I really need that coffee this morning." Rick was a regular here and knew many of the servers by name.

"The sandwich will take a couple of minutes," Amy said with a smile. "Just take your usual seat and I will bring it over when it's ready"

"Excellent," he responded as he took the much-needed coffee with him to a seat at the back of the restaurant. The sun was bright and the table was flooded with warm rays as he sat waiting for the food. It was a nice change from his previous few visits that had been on cool and dreary days.

His usual table hadn't been cleared since the previous diners had sat there. Left behind were two untouched children's coloring pages of a sunflower and one red crayon. Rick looked down at the lifeless black-and-white images of the sunflower on the coloring page. Then he glanced at the single red crayon. "Hmm, these will be kind of crappy pictures with only one color for such a pretty flower," he thought as he started to fill the first one in.

By the time the food arrived, he had completed coloring the stem, petals and flower, all in red. He had stayed between the lines and the consistency was perfect, but it was a single, boring red flower. "It doesn't even look like a sunflower," he thought as he surveyed his handiwork. He reflected on a recent family trip to Tuscany and the seemingly endless sea of beautiful sunflowers in vibrant yellows and greens that he had observed along the highway outside Siena, Italy. His was not an inspirational flower at all.

Setting Rick's breakfast sandwich on the table, Amy glanced at his artistry and jokingly commented, "Well done, young man. But don't you know what a sunflower looks like in real life?"

Rick held up his single red crayon and said forlornly, "This was my only tool. It's hard to create art with only one red crayon." He laughed.

"That was your first mistake," she laughed and went back to the counter.

He began to eat the sandwich and thought about Amy's final comment. He became curious what she meant by it and went back to the counter to ask her for more detail. Amy saw him coming up and reached under the counter to grab something. Rick laughed to himself that she was probably signaling the police, but she pulled up a cup filled with many different colored crayons.

"Here you are, young fella. All the colors of the rainbow," she smirked.

Rick took the crayons and said, "Thanks, these should make a big difference. Tell me, though, why did you say, 'That was your first mistake?' What did you mean by that, exactly?"

Amy laughed and said that she was an art student and she knew that it was difficult to capture the essence of something with only one color or even a single medium. Not impossible, but very difficult. "Besides," she added, "it's pretty risky to work in only one color or one medium, with just one tool. I mean, the scope of the work will be very limited. You will miss vital and subtle dynamics of the content you are trying to communicate. Moreover, it won't appeal to many—unless they really, really, *really* like red-crayon drawings."

"So, what you meant was that expertise in a singular medium may not be suitable for every situation or problem," suggested Rick.

"Well, I was talking about the crayon," clarified Amy. "Different colors and media will really make that picture interesting. A variety of tools allows the viewer to see the nuances the artist intended to capture and reveal. Instead of bashing the whole thing red. A richer and more diversified technique might even reveal something else within the subject, something you wished it could be but wasn't quite yet. Why do you ask?"

"I feel that expertise can often lead to a form of tunnel-vision that really limits creative solutions," said Rick. "Don't get me wrong, expertise is vital, but it can result in a form of . . . " He was cut off by Amy jumping in.

"Groupthink?"

"Yeah," replied Rick. "Almost. For example, a person may meet an advisor and describe his situation. The advisor, using her checklists and expertise, provides an answer from her particular perspective. But what if the real problem was elsewhere in the facts? What if she, the advisor, didn't or couldn't recognize that the core issue was much more complicated and needed the skills and perspective of a different professional?" mused Rick aloud.

"You might get a great answer to the wrong question," said Amy.

Amy had to attend to another customer who had appeared, and Rick apologized and went back to his table. He wolfed down the sandwich and absent-mindedly used the other crayons to color the second sunflower. He was gazing out the window into the park when Amy returned to clear the plate and refresh his coffee mug.

"I was thinking about our discussion just now," she said. As she spoke, she picked up the red crayon drawing. "Did you ever read about Steve Jobs and what he brought to Apple?"

"I know he was a perfectionist about many things," said Rick. "Part P. T. Barnum and part Nikola Tesla."

"Yeah, I'm not sure who those guys are," said Amy. "But Jobs believed that design and function could come together to create beautiful tools in life. He understood that people wanted to love the look and feel of what they used, like a computer or a phone. He researched German Bauhaus art design and traveled the world to bring extra dimensions to the user experience with products. He was an innovator because he was able to fuse the best ideas of other fields into one beautifully designed product. He wanted to create an overall experience, not just a mechanical tool."

Rick stared at her for a moment. She had hit a nail on the head. The coloring he had done on the first sunflower was the simplest possible outcome with a single perspective. He asked her, "Do you think it's possible to bring design to any type of planning, to incorporate essential real beauty, elegance and functionality?"

She pondered for a moment and then said, "Well, if you could, people would likely buy it. It would stand out from the crowd and probably get people more engaged. As opposed to this monochrome crimson abomination." Glancing down at the table, she noticed the second, more colorful, sunflower Rick had completed. "This one is much more realistic but still kind of pedestrian," she laughed as she picked them both up for comparison. "You're getting closer to a better picture, but you're not there yet."

She was about to rip up the images when Rick interjected, "Whoa, whoa . . . don't tear those up. I'm going to keep them as mementos of our conversation today," he laughed.

"All right, young man," she chuckled, "it was nice talking to you."

"Why do you keep calling me 'young fella' and 'young man?'" asked Rick. "You're half my age."

"You were the one coloring with crayons, not me." She smiled as she walked away.

• • •

Rick headed back to the office. He was now more convinced than ever that a multidisciplinary strategic approach was the best way to bring elegant design and technical functionality into a single plan. He grabbed a decaffeinated coffee in the building food court and returned to his office to ponder this new revelation.

At his desk, he reviewed his conference journal and started to type out his various thoughts and the important points his reflections had brought forward. It was time to start organizing these concepts into a coherent process. He began to type.

- Tax planning is a poor starting point for wealth management or wealth-continuity planning.
- Estate and wealth planning are really about continuity planning for the longer term.
- A strategic approach is essential. Tactical solutions are troublesome starting points.
- Families must identify and agree upon their core sources of family wealth—financial, social, human and intellectual.
- Without a goal, the ship of family wealth management lacks a rudder.
- Single-subject expertise is insufficient.
- Strategic planning is hard work and requires deliberate practice for families.
- Tactic-based planning ensures the wealth of families is destroyed between generations.
- The need to preserve wealth has never been more economically

vital.

- A multidisciplinary, growth-oriented mindset is required for transition success—coloring in one hue misses the real story that needs to be revealed.
- Skills in communication, governance and conflict resolution are essential to the continuity of family wealth;
- Avoiding poor decisions and biases in decision-making is important to sustaining wealth.

Rick leaned back and thought to himself, "Okay, these are all important, but where is the starting point for this approach? How can I build this process into steps that clients and advisors can replicate and use for themselves?"

He pondered for a time on his list. He tried to order and regroup them on a priority basis. It was difficult and just trying to identify a logical process was a challenge. He realized how hard it must be for clients who have the added emotional components of their own reality to manage as well.

As he reflected, he decided that a good place to start was the beginning. The start of any journey or process usually has a *why*. A problem has presented itself or an opportunity for action has arisen. Why do we care how this ends? Why should we start down this path? What are we really hoping to achieve from this endeavor? The starting point of any strategic process was to identify goals and that means identifying the *why* in any situation.

"Effectively answering those questions will require a process of decision-making and option assessment," Rick thought. "An effective governance model will be needed and that model has to always be asking "Why?" Understanding the why is really about appreciating and nurturing the values of an individual or family. If I can identify and articulate a family's core value system, then I can help them find their why and start to authentically create their governance and communication framework. It is about setting goals that achieve the why and building strategies to achieve those goals." This was clearly going to be a deep-diving, time-consuming and difficult process. "Which is probably why it rarely ever gets done," Rick thought.

"Still," he ruminated, "individuals, families and companies all set goals. There is a way to do this and be successful." To facilitate goal-setting and a strategic focus, some families create mission statements, much like many successful companies do. Every traveler benefits from recognizable compass points or reference to a pole star to stay true on a journey. Rick decided that a thoughtful and purposefully created mission statement would help to keep the destination in focus. That was an important element for his new process: creating a family mission statement.

He recalled that several speakers at Convergence agreed that family mission statements were foundational documents for successful intergenerational wealth continuity. He checked his conference notebook for the day-two presentation Angela had introduced. "Yes, here it is," he said as he found the section. He picked up a blue highlighter and marked the key sections:

- Family mission statement process functions to engage the next generation
- Working together ensures next generation commitment to process and purpose
- Captures family's broader values and intentions
- Collective vision enhances engagement
- Sets a virtuous circle in motion
- Increases likelihood of strategic planning success

After reviewing his notes, Rick typed out:

A family mission statement is used to bring alignment of focus, purpose and action among family members in relation to their collective values and broader family goals over the longer term.

"Interestingly, this definition is both aspirational and actionable," he mused. "It's a statement that will be acted upon when the goals and objectives of the family are articulated in their intergenerational wealth-continuity plan. Every member of the family should feel the *gravitas* of the mission statement in their actions, words and choices. The planning process itself also creates a virtuous circle of definition and purposeful clarity because the mission statement will be regularly refined as goals are articulated and experience is gained working towards those goals."

Just then, Rick's friend Auston, the financial planner, popped his head in the door. "Working hard, Rick, or hardly working?" he asked.

Rick rolled his eyes and responded, "The answer, as always, is it depends."

"Damned lawyers," chuckled Auston. "You won't even definitively answer a joke question. What are you working on?"

Rick explained his ideas and how he wanted to build a process model that offered starting points for advisors and clients to do better planning. He explained how he was thinking that a family mission statement was a good entry point into a strategic model.

"You have likely considered this already," started Auston, "but I feel the biggest impediment to good planning is lack of communication; and, conversely, a significant contributor to powerful planning is effective family communication. I would maybe step back and change your starting point a little."

"Thank you," said Rick. "That's a great insight. I always dive right into the solution. I am trying to manage that reflex. However, people need to start somewhere that builds good habits for the rest of the journey. Families will really benefit from understanding how to start this process and this conversation."

"Exactly," agreed Auston. "They take it for granted that they have the ability to generate these ideas and discuss them in a meaningful way that will lead to successful results. But they usually don't have an effective communication approach at all. Especially as they begin to grow as a family and experience more emotional, dynamic and complex situations such as business-transition planning or wealth-continuity planning. If this were my model, I would suggest that they spend some time practicing effective communications by holding a sequence of family meetings."

"In a purposeful manner," interjected Rick.

"Meaning?" asked Auston.

"Meaning," explained Rick, "that one of the outcomes of family meetings is to develop communication skills and mastery within the family itself. Deepening those skills will ensure that unnecessary energy is not spent on interpreting motivations and intent with words. The family will have a process they can use to honestly and safely bring ideas forth and address them. It's really a type of pre-conflict resolution tool."

"That's a better starting point," agreed Auston. "The advisor needs to see how the family communicates on decisions. Who gets heard? Who doesn't? How do they decide? Is it collaborative or autocratic? Do they understand the differences and what types of communications would they like to build for their own process?"

"It should also be a process that is authentic to the family," added Rick. "After all, it's their voices."

"Yes, and it's important that they appreciate the potential and the limits of their existing communication styles," said Auston. "Bigger and tougher decisions may require adoption of more robust sharing of information and debate. That's a skill that can be learned and it helps to facilitate the success of the process itself."

"That's a vital insight," said Rick. "The success of this model is very much a product of effective communication and decision-making."

"After all: shit in, shit out," laughed Auston.

"How pithy and elegant at the same time," chuckled Rick. "Okay, step one is assessing and developing some skills with communication and decision-making. I think one way to do that is to have a series of family meetings to model and then create that process architecture."

"That may take some time," said Auston. "You don't want to rush that."

"Agreed," said Rick. "And there is a lot of literature available on conducting family meetings to get people started. The first few steps of this process should be about building trust in the process itself."

To that, Auston replied, "I would suggest that a facilitator be considered to help them through the initial stages of creating a meeting framework to appreciate their existing communication styles and to experience and adopt new approaches if they are appropriate."

"I got ahead of myself there a bit," said Rick. "Not every family will be at ease going it alone on creating communication skills. It's so vital to be successful at this stage . . ."

"Before any complex and emotional concepts are introduced into the fray," interjected Auston. "Communication skills are essential because they smooth the process of successfully transitioning information and they help to develop relational strength between the communicating parties."

Rick nodded in agreement and continued. "If they do it right, they simply get to know one another more deeply and accurately. Okay, so to summarize: family meetings and the development of useful communication skills are the first steps in this process. I think the next step should be something everyone can get behind; an item on which there will be broad agreement and alignment. You know, something that builds trust, creates energy and, in the process, allows for practice in effective communication and decision-making."

"I would think that's where your values-oriented mission statement would fit the bill perfectly," suggested Auston.

"You have given this some thought already," laughed Rick.

"As we discussed earlier, I like to use a goals orientation in my financial planning," said Auston. "This is very relevant to the work I do. Values and goals are foundational to sustainable planning. I love that you are building a way to bring some linearity to these concepts. You know, where to start and how to move forward."

Rick nodded his appreciation for the kind words and made a mental note that Auston, a millennial, was intrinsically accepting of a values-centered and goals-based strategic approach to planning.

This would be powerful intelligence for his future work with second-generation family members and younger professional advisors.

"I guess I might be confused about how a mission statement is different from a strategic approach. Is it different?" asked Auston.

Rick pondered the question for a moment and then spoke. "Creating a mission statement means identifying shared family values. It's not so much different from a strategic approach as it is an early step along the strategic path. These values are then discussed and prioritized and filtered into a cohesive narrative form upon which action can be directed. The mission statement will reveal broad methods of living, protecting and respecting those values."

Auston picked up on the distinction. "So, really, they aren't distinct steps as much as they are points along a planning continuum. The strategic approach is baked into the continuum itself."

"Hmm . . . that is a bit confusing," said Rick. "I need to clarify that. You are correct, though. But maybe I need some terminology that takes away the confusion."

"Here's a thought," said Auston. "Why not call the whole process something different? You know, rather than just calling it a strategic model. It's a model that will use a strategic approach, but it has other elements."

"Despite the rumors, Auston, you are smart. I have been toying with calling it simply the Abundant Estate. What do you think?" asked Rick.

"Well, despite the insult, it's a good idea," said Auston. "Why did you choose that name? The Abundant Estate?"

Rick paused to reflect and then said with a smile, "Most of our planning is based on resource scarcity. We plan to conserve and preserve. This changes the mentality of all the participants and stakeholders in the plan. However, I think we should plan with an abundance mindset. Families are rich with sources of wealth that can be deliberately nurtured and developed to create abundance. We should adopt a view that our family wealth is a source of growth and possibility rather than a pool of dissipating value."

"Wow," said Auston. "That's really different. You would tend to view estate planning as a source of opportunity rather than entropy. Creation versus destruction."

"Exactly," Rick continued. "Because it becomes a lifelong process of stewardship to grow and nurture rather than to hoard and waste. It's fundamentally optimistic about human potential, but with a process in mind."

"So, the Abundant Estate is an approach that incorporates strategy. But, it's an approach that must start somewhere and . . . ." he trailed off.

"And the beginning is the best place to start," finished Rick. "After establishing communication skills through family meetings, identifying shared core values is the beginning of a mission statement. The values are also the basis of planning alignment. A value is a touchstone of definition for a person and a group. If something doesn't align with a value, it can be discarded."

"Okay," said Auston. "And the mission statement is the action-oriented version of those various core values. Is that reasonable?"

"Yes," replied Rick. "Does that make sense to you?"

"It does now. I suppose the question for the next steps is how do mission and strategy come together? In what order? Or, is there even an order?" asked Auston.

Rick pondered this for a moment. It was a good question.

Auston continued. "I think what you are suggesting is, there are many ways to do this and that your process is just one method that will work. They can add to it by re-ordering, mixing and matching along the way. They can make it fit their needs to some extent. It can be organic to their family," he finished, checking his watch.

"Yes, that's it," said Rick. "It's like a best practice in a way. But I don't like calling it that."

"I agree, "said Auston. "That's a limiting term. Successful practices are very idiosyncratic. What's best for one group could be terrible for another. The important thing is to start at your beginning and decide what you want to do . . . then build and continuously adapt a process around that. Is that a fair statement?" he asked, again checking his watch.

"You need to go?" asked Rick.

"I have a meeting downstairs in five minutes. You are on to something, Ricker," said Auston on his way out.

After he departed, Rick thought about Auston's final statement: start at your beginning and decide what you want to do, then build and continuously adapt a process around that. "My approach can serve as a good guide to keep that in focus," he thought to himself. "Once the skills of effective meetings are mastered and values have been identified, the mission statement is a great next step. It's fundamentally about values and vision. What the family wants to do next is executed or carried out through the strategic decision-making process that follows. That's the point where I will begin to model strategy development."

Continuing with this train of thought, Rick mused, "Once the family has gotten underway with good meetings, they will want to monument some of their shared beliefs, values and key observations. The elements they value and like become the building blocks of how they will share information and interact as a family."

It occurred to Rick that the participants could also discuss the various methods of decision-making that exist in their family, such as autocratic, consensus, democratic and collaborative. "Maybe some decisions are better made democratically rather than collaboratively," he pondered. For example, the decision to act on a particular tactic may suggest that everyone actually affected by the choice has an equal vote on the matter.

In fact, Rick had just that week met a business family that was struggling to move ownership and management from the founder generation to the rising next generation. Although it was an initial meeting, he immediately recognized that a core challenge was going to be the transition from how decisions were presently made versus into the future. The business founder was a benevolent dictator. He sought input but made the final decision on everything of importance. He maintained the ultimate veto power and this was reinforced in the corporate share structure. However, he also had several children in senior leadership positions. They were responsible, respected and wanted a voice in their future. The founder was struggling with how to transfer that authority but, more importantly, he wasn't coping well with his own apparent reduction of power. As a result, he was resisting change and his oldest daughter was now seriously contemplating a job offer with another firm where she could exert real leadership authority. It was a crisis moment for the family and the business. It seemed to Rick that learning how to share some internal decision-making, in order to bilaterally build trust, might be a good place to start for this family.

As he reflected on that meeting, he thought, "The benevolent dictator model of decision-making has been in place since the founder started the business. Yet, many other family decisions are likely made using more democratic approaches."

Rick thought about how, in his own family, he'd lost a winter vacation vote 3–1 last year, meaning they went to Walt Disney World instead of Hawaii. That was okay with him, but it was only a vote about a family trip, it wasn't a business or ownership decision. Every situation in which a choice is required has its own architecture that is accepted by the stakeholders until it isn't accepted anymore. That's when a transformation is needed, and managing that change is critical. In family businesses, the evolution from founder to the rising generation presents transitional points where decision-making models need modification. Engaged family wealth-continuity planning was no different.

He continued in his thinking. "Families and their advisors often hear the word 'communication' and roll their eyes. 'Of course we communicate, we are family,' is their immediate response." He then reflected on how he communicated within his own family. "Sometimes I am Dad and sometimes I am husband. Because we have a family business, I often communicate both as a shareholder and a manager. It's very dynamic and complex. Identical words can be interpreted very differently depending on the perspective of the listener about which hat I am wearing when the words are spoken."

Rick was reminded of an anecdote that a business owner once shared with him about keeping the spheres of family and business well-delineated. The business owner had a son in the operation who was a total disaster as an employee. The other staff were complaining all the time and morale was slipping. Some key employees were known to be looking elsewhere for work. One night, the business owner called his son into his home office and had two hats on his desk.

"Why do you have a hat marked 'Boss' and one marked 'Dad?'" asked his son.

The business owner put on his Boss hat and said, "Billy, your effort at work is terrible and despite all our efforts to remediate the situation, you continue to struggle. I have no choice but you let you go immediately."

Startled, the son asked, "Well, what's the deal with the Dad hat?"

The father took off the Boss hat and put on the Dad cap. He got up, came around the desk and hugged his son and said, "I heard you lost your job today, son. This will be a very challenging time for you. Do you want to talk about it over a beer?"

Communication, or information sharing, is enhanced when everyone understands the source, perspective and voice that is actually speaking. To that end, good process helps ensure the intended voice and message are properly received and interpreted. Process also supports content because even a great message will be lost if no one is listening or there is no purposeful engagement. Family meetings are the starting point and forum for developing a mission statement. The family meeting was the backbone of the process.

Rick decided to chronicle some of the reasons family meetings and communication were essential:

1. To foster a culture supportive of sustainable intergenerational wealth transfer

2. To engage family philanthropy

3. To promote family financial literacy and education

4. To create and enhance the effectiveness of family governance

"I want families to build a good communication process for themselves," he thought to himself. "This process will yield authentic mission statements and better decision-making, not only throughout the planning process but also in the ongoing governance and stewardship of family wealth." He began typing some questions to consider as a family starts down that path:

1. Who will be entitled to participate in our family meetings? What voice will they have in those meetings?

2. Are all voices equal on all issues in a meeting?

3. How often will we meet?

4. Will we make use of committees?

5. Where will we meet?

6. Who will take charge of the logistics and be responsible for agendas and scheduling?

7. What method of communication will we use to share information?

8. What information will we share? With everyone?

9. What if there is disagreement?

10. What decision-making approaches will we use? Majority rule? Tiered voting?

11. Should a facilitator be engaged to model best practices for conducting a meeting?

12. Should we reduce our decisions to a Meeting Code of Conduct and Family Communications Protocol?

He recalled one presenter at the San Diego conference commenting that "formality is your friend" in these circumstances. Rick agreed with this. Having a set of rules meant expectations could be created around fair process and shared issue resolution. "It also creates a safe and productive space," he mused. "Members know how to introduce a matter, how it will be discussed and the repercussions of raising the flag after the fact. A reciprocal and healthy communication system built with authenticity and engagement is also sustaining for the process itself."

Rick pondered this idea some more. "I loved the concept of schismogenesis that was discussed in San Diego. If one person is holding back information and another perceives this, they will also hold back information. It is a communication death spiral that guarantees the decisions made will be damaging to the entire family, business and management ecosystem. Transparency, honesty and clarity are vital. The process must always work to create and enhance those features."

His brain now pulling it all together, Rick thought to himself, "After the family has spent some time developing effective communication, using a meeting cycle to identify shared core values is the logical next step. From there, the third step is to develop the shared values into an actionable family mission statement. The fourth step is significant in scope and effort. It will be the multi-phase and ongoing strategic process." He was getting excited to see his model emerge.

Just then, Auston stopped by and knocked on the office window, "Jeez, you're right where I left you an hour ago," he said. "What's your job description, again?"

Rick laughed and asked what happened in the meeting.

"I was presenting a plan," Auston said. "It's funny, they didn't seem too interested until I started talking about their ability to fund their charitable goals. Then they lit up. They were arguing a bit with one another. That's why I am done so early. They wanted to talk about it more."

"Just not in front of you," laughed Rick.

Auston laughed and added, "They could use some help tracking through this issue. Not the technical aspect, that's the easy part. But the decision-making process over starting, running and sustaining the fund. That's where they are struggling. Lots of concerns over legacy and family values messaging."

"Not the sort of answers one finds in a financial plan, I suspect," smiled Rick.

"Not typically," replied Auston. "They are grappling with deeper, family identity decisions. They don't have a process to deal with their concerns in an effective manner, and it's compromising their decision-making efforts. There is just too much emotion."

Rick took a moment to summarize his efforts since they had last spoken, and Auston took note of the coincidence and prescience of their conversations. He suggested they grab a couple of dark roasts so they could continue their conversation. Rick agreed and disconnected his laptop. They traveled to the main floor café area to talk further.

As they sat down in the café with their coffees, Rick said, "Collecting and chronicling the shared beliefs and values of the family is a crucial early step in the process."

"Agreed," said Auston. "If this gets done right, it should be an enjoyable process of sharing reflections on what it means to be a member of this family. A healthy, nurturing and growth-oriented culture is essential in any organization, including a family. I can't think of any business, be it a not-for-profit or a family business, that has succeeded long-term while ignoring the health of its internal culture."

Rick nodded his agreement and added, "Internal matters eventually manifest themselves externally. Long-term success means taking the time to get it right early and understanding the strengths and weaknesses of the family. The shared values and beliefs are like the glue that keeps people together."

"As I hear you say it, I don't like the glue metaphor, Rick," said Auston. "It makes me think of people as unwanted rodents that are trapped. Stickiness is a dangerous metaphor."

"You completely missed your calling," laughed Rick. "You are absolutely right. Family members have bonds, but they should never feel stuck."

"It's a choice," said Auston. "A destination of choice—of affinity, really. They have shared history, experiences and values that bring them together, but they stay together by choice. The bonds of affinity also keep them together because the benefits can be so demonstrably significant. That's a very, very different model to build around."

Rick nodded his agreement. "I have noticed that many consultants and advisors just focus on the negatives with families. You know, 'Let's address the risks and threats first.' In the process, they often ignore the family's strengths. I mean, it seems to me that the strengths are sources of sustainability and meaning. We should encourage investment in those aspects at least as much as the threats, if not much more."

They sipped their coffees in silence for a moment pondering the gravity of that concept.

Auston broke the silence. "You know, in the many years I have been doing this work, I have never once suggested that a client consider a strategy to invest their financial wealth in the identifiable strengths of their family. I always look to plan for the negatives and mitigate risk."

"Me too, I am afraid," added Rick. "We all focus primarily on avoiding negatives, almost never on investing in the positives. How could I have missed that? I mean . . . ." he trailed off.

"If we don't help people with this, who will?" asked Auston. "You know, this model you are developing really triggers a series of personal revelations. We're talking about it, and it has brought us to the realization of just how deficient we are in the work we do. We could achieve so much more. Families will have these epiphanies as well. Let's keep going."

Rick opened his laptop and began recording the key aspects of their conversation. They agreed that family members can consider many self-reflection and self-identification questions, including:

1. What does being a member of this family mean to me?

2. What does being a member of this family mean to the communities to which we belong?

3. What do I like best about being a member of this family?

4. What are the strengths this family demonstrates in business and the community?

5. What family stories do I enjoy the most? What is the reason I like that story best of all? What is the message of that story?

6. In moments of stress or crisis, what family members impressed and inspired me most, and how did they do that?

7. What family traditions do I most enjoy? What do those traditions that I like best reveal about this family?

8. How has being a member of this family made me a better person?

9. What makes our family unique from other families I have observed?

10. What values are central to our family's story? Do we want to preserve these values?

"A series of family meetings could pass through some or all of these inquiries, until family members arrive at a comfort level and a readiness to explore their personal and shared values. Identifying the shared or most common values will lead to a wide-ranging and in-depth discussion of the various values themselves, which creates a virtuous cycle of introspection," said Rick.

"In that process," added Auston, "the definitions and parameters of the values will be debated and established. It has tremendous utility, in addition to being the eventual basis of a family mission statement."

"It's important to commit some meeting cycles to creating these skills," added Rick.

"What do you mean by meeting cycles?" asked Auston.

"Well," started Rick. "It might take two meetings or ten meetings, maybe more, before the necessary skills have been developed to move forward with any steps in this process. Families may need to experience a series of meetings to fully address these matters. They should be very wary of moving ahead until the requirements of a specific step have been fulfilled. The cycle would consist of however many meetings are required before they can take the next full step forward in the Abundant Estate process."

"Okay," Auston jumped in. "Let's talk about values now."

They decided to prepare a short list of common values as examples.

"We could use this list to help them differentiate between a value and a characteristic or preference," said Rick.

"How would you make that distinction?" asked Auston.

"Well, some people say you are clever and witty," started Rick.

"Just some?" asked Auston.

"Just some," smirked Rick. "But, cleverness and wittiness aren't really core values. They are traits or features of your personality. If I asked a few more questions to probe deeper, I would likely discover that your cleverness and wittiness emerge from wisdom. So, what people really like is the wisdom that emerges from your expressions of wit and cleverness. Does that make sense? They value your wisdom. You just happen to express that through your wit and clever responses. "

Auston indicated that he understood, and Rick continued.

"Characteristics and preferences are more matters of personality from one person to the next rather than shared core family values," added Rick as he typed out a short list of examples of values that a family may collectively hold dear:

- Beauty
- Wisdom
- Grace
- Humility
- Loyalty
- Legacy

"That's a good starting point," said Auston. "If they get stuck about what is revealed in their answers, we can plumb that obstacle more deeply."

Rick recalled attending a session on creating business and family mission statements at the Convergence conference in San Diego. He had recorded his notes on his iPhone. Accessing the notes on the cloud now, he shared the screen with Auston and commented, "One of the takeaways from that conference was that effective mission statements often reveal these components about the family."

Auston chuckled. "Takeaways . . . speak normal English, man. That's my ask."

Both laughed as they looked at Rick's conference notes under the heading "Mission Statements Reveal":

1. Aligned values

2. Shared beliefs

3. Desired levels of, and methods for, information sharing

4. Expectations around family engagement

5. Commitment to purposeful change

"Commitment to purposeful change was a paraphrase on my part," Rick recalled. "That session was about taking steps to move forward with action. But, as I reflected on it in more detail, I preferred purposeful action rather than simply action. Just doing stuff is a problem the Abundant Estate will try to resolve. People confuse action with effective results. Purposeful action is a commitment to change, not just for the sake of change but because it drives purpose for those who will be affected by the planning."

As he and Auston pondered this more deeply, Rick realized that a commitment to purposeful change was the linchpin from the mission statement to the strategic process. He shared this with Auston and added, "It's a way of saying, 'Okay, we have this mission, now what process are we going to use to give effect to it? How do we go from agreeing upon what makes us great and worth staying together as a group to action dedicated to sustaining that mission?'"

As Rick said this, he thought to himself, "That will be resolved at the multi-level fourth step of the Abundant Estate process."

Rick and Auston continued to brainstorm and decided that a short list of threshold considerations would be helpful to start the conversation.

"The average person has no idea where to begin when creating a family mission statement," said Auston.

"Agreed," said Rick. "And we don't want the process to be still-born. We are building a road map for people; a process model to start them on their journey forward." He started to type a summary of their thoughts:

- **Be sincere**—Make sure everyone is engaged and understands the purpose and benefit of the process.
- **Be together**—Consensus will build authenticity; take the time to seek input from as many family members as possible.
- **Be original**—Don't use another family's mission statement; it needs to be authentic to your family.
- **Be patient**—It's a marathon and not a sprint. This process is hard work; consider a neutral facilitator or family enterprise consultant to coordinate the process and model good practices. Effective facilitation also promotes good communication.

"That makes a handy little acronym," said Rick. "Before you dig into this process, take time to STOP and make sure you are proceeding in a manner that will enhance success."

"Clever for a law-talking guy," said Auston. "It's pretty typical to try and see what other people have done before you start something. But that often bakes in inauthentic considerations and ideas. It's better to create your own mission statement without reference to another family's version. It forces you to consider the distinctiveness of your collective experience and direction."

"That's a lot of ground covered," said Rick as they both got up to return to the office.

Auston added, "This is hard work for families, and they'll need guidance and deliberate practice to achieve success. This isn't the kind of thing you bang out in two meetings."

"Moreover, the information collected may be full of seemingly insurmountable paradoxes and changes in power dynamics that must be managed," said Rick, as they stepped onto the elevator. "But like most things that are a challenge to master, the rewards can be enormous and enduring."

• • •

Back in his office, Rick reflected on how the day had, so far, been a creative success. With Auston's help, he had organized and transferred a lot of discrete concepts, theory and experience into an evolving model people could actually use. He was very excited to start engaging this tool with his own clients to better their wealth-continuity planning and make real change in their lives.

His morning of creativity had been fueled in part with copious amounts of Kona coffee. Kona was his favorite coffee, and he really liked that aspect of the creative process—lots of excuses for coffee. The problem with coffee though, as with beer, is that you cannot own the product, you can only rent it. He urgently headed off to the washroom deep in thought over his evolving strategic model and how and when it would be best to introduce this to his professional work.

Exiting the washroom, he ran into a colleague, Jim Fox. Jim was an investment advisor with a reputation in the office for fairness and scrupulous honesty. Older now, he had managed to survive the industry's transition from the stock brokerage model to fee-based wealth management.

"Can I bend your ear about a client for a moment?" Jim asked Rick.

"Sure, Jim," Rick replied. He was surprised. Jim had never consulted him or other planning colleagues about his clients.

They went into Jim's office and shut the door. The spartan space offered a great view of the city and a vantage point that allowed for unparalleled vistas when thunderstorms and winter squalls blew in from the west. No storms today, though, as the sun shone brilliantly into their eyes.

"What's up, Jim?" asked Rick. He fully expected a question about the probate process, how to shave a few dollars in tax or some tale of a borderline-hilarious family law entanglement of some client.

"Well," Jim started, "I have a client situation. His name is Doug Matthews. I'm not sure where to start. They have a large family business. It may be in transition, I'm not sure. There are two children and, I am somewhat embarrassed to admit, his new wife is someone I have not dealt with very much over the last few years. Doug and I always worked with only one another. The whole plan was he would eventually monetize his business and then I would manage the post-sale assets."

Rick was unfazed that Jim, Doug's long-time advisor, had so little knowledge of the full depth of the complete family situation. For a variety of reasons, many professional advisors had only surface-level knowledge of their clients' deeper personal and business affairs. This was not very unusual. But it was unusual to admit it.

"How can I help?" Rick asked.

"Well," Jim stammered, "they have been approached by another firm called Holistic Financial. They offered to do a financial plan and develop some legal and estate structures. I have reviewed some of the early output and it seems impressive. Doug and Sarah wondered why I had never discussed these services with them over the years. And, frankly . . . I really had no good answer."

"How far along in the process have they actually gone with Holistic?" asked Rick.

"They led with a life insurance review and they are trying to set up meetings to do a financial plan and estate review," Jim answered.

"Tell me what you know about this client," requested Rick. He thought that it may still be possible to rescue this situation.

"Doug entered the business, it's called ScrapCo, about twenty-five years ago," said Jim as he began the tale. "It was a manufacturing business, although that has changed over the years. He does about

$10 million a year in sales and is a really good saver. I have about $2 million of his wealth but none of Sarah's money."

"Sarah?" queried Rick.

"Sorry, Doug's second wife. Gabrielle, his first wife, died of cancer quite a few years back. I don't have a lot of contact with Sarah. She was married before, but I don't recall what happened there. I think she was divorced from her first husband . . . maybe . . . I don't really recall," a visibly flustered Jim responded.

"Okay, second marriage, this will be good. If people could ever figure out how to manage their personal affairs in an orderly manner, the legal profession would compress by half overnight," Rick laughed to himself.

"Does he have children and are they in the business?" he asked Jim.

"There are two children. Todd is for sure in the business. He is the heir apparent to the enterprise, I would say. His sister used to work at ScrapCo in the summers during school but has since left town and lives in Hawaii," said Jim.

"Wow, she *really* left town," smiled Rick, trying to lighten the mood. "Tell me, what you do know about their situation? Did they do a marriage contract?" asked Rick.

"I have no idea," said Jim. "Probably not, she has no real interest in the business."

"How do you know she has no interest in the business?" asked Rick. "Did you canvas that topic?" He already knew the answer.

"Well, I am assuming a little bit there, I guess," Jim stammered.

"Updated wills?" asked Rick.

"No clue, really," replied Jim. "I know who his lawyer is, I went to university with him. But no, I have no real idea on that kind of stuff. I don't really like to ask. It's very personal and sometimes people don't like to talk about it. He is financially successful, so more than likely his wills and tax situation are very well cared for."

"We should never make that assumption," said Rick. "I will send a few dates, let's arrange to meet this client," added Rick. "I'll make up a list of information I need and we will really take a deep dive into the facts in this case. Let's see what's there."

"That would be great," said Jim. "My real concern is that the eventual sale of the business translates well for Doug for tax reasons. He is all about tax savings and is always pounding me to do the most efficient tax planning possible. He's a tough client to manage but I have his trust and respect. He has had really good investment returns over the years."

Rick listened to Jim's words and was reminded of the Gumble meeting he'd had before he went to the Convergence conference. That meeting was driven by tax planning, and purposeful planning was shut down by an emphasis on tactics over strategy. It was the type of meeting and process he swore he would never allow to happen again. Jim didn't know it yet, but he was about to be the first advisor, along with his clients, to experience Rick's evolving Abundant Estate model—all fueled by Rick having ingested a whole lot of Kona coffee before noon.

"Well," started Rick, "tax is certainly a place we will go, but it's not likely the place we will start. I may not get there until the end, whether he likes it or not."

Jim was visibly nervous about that response. "I am pretty sure that's all that will be of interest to him. He's all about the tax. It has been the constant theme over the years," he confidently added.

"Did he start this business himself?" asked Rick, changing the subject.

"Sort of," answered Jim. "It was his dad's. He took it over out of university and transformed it from a small shop into a large operation. He's a smart guy; he studied engineering at university."

"Well, we will talk to him and get the lay of the land," Rick said, trying to maintain control of the process. "My experience is that many clients who own businesses seek external help and advice but are only minimally aware of their real issues. They know something is bugging them, but they aren't sure how to describe it, let alone fix it. As a result, they either stop asking the questions or they rephrase them in some manner. Sometimes they quickly glom onto a technical response because it feels like action. They don't like to plan much, business owners. This will potentially be some hard work for all of us. Did he ask you about these services, or did you mention them to him?"

"Sarah told him they were available," Jim responded. "She saw them on our website and sent me an e-mail asking for more information about estate planning and business succession planning. When I got the e-mail, I called Doug up and that's when I found out that this whole thing was going on with the other financial services firm."

Jim's response had inadvertently divulged a lot of information about the depth of his interactions with this client. It was clear he really didn't have any relationship with the new spouse. Jim and the lawyer probably had long-term relationships with Jim's first wife, and Sarah was likely perceived as an interloper to the family enterprise ecosystem. Her arrival heralded a disruption of communication and power in all the relationships. The lack of connection put the entire business relationship at risk—if not today, then when Doug died.

The call to Doug when Sarah e-mailed was likely a poor choice. It simply reinforced the real basis of their relationship with Jim. The e-mail was a signal from Sarah that she was engaged and interested. She wanted information. While it was possible that the situation was stable and healthy, it was also possible that she had been excluded from conversations about money and business. More discovery was needed to reveal the truth before any solution could be safely suggested. However, Rick sensed that Jim was open to exploring his relationship with this client family.

Jim circled back to Rick's earlier comment. "What did you mean when you said that tax might not be the starting point? I know it will be the main point of interest for Doug. Like I said, he hates paying taxes."

"Jim, most people are trained early to see taxation minimization as the only reason to plan," Rick explained. "But let's take a closer look from his perspective: second marriage, deceased first wife, kids in and out of the business and Doug near retirement age. Frankly, I suspect he has a lot on his mind. My hunch is that we will find this isn't about tax at all. He's reaching around for help with bigger issues. I bet he is somewhat lost for direction for the first time in his life. The fact that Sarah started the ball rolling and Doug kept it in play is very revealing."

"How do you mean?" asked Jim.

"Well, she sent the initial e-mail, right?" asked Rick.

"Yes, and I immediately called Doug. What's your point?" asked a frustrated Jim.

"Well, why did you call him?" asked Rick. "She was the one who reached out. Who should be your client here?"

Jim thought for a moment and said sheepishly, "Okay. That was Neanderthal of me. I should have called her back or at least arranged to speak to them both together about her request. The family should be my client, I suppose. I know him best, though. But why do you find her request and his response revealing?"

"Well, my suspicion—and I obviously don't know much about these folks at all—is that Doug is used to calling the shots around the business. It's also probable that his first wife ran the home front. Yet, his new spouse reached out on his behalf and asked about business succession planning and estate planning. Think about that for a minute, Jim. Is that different from in the past?" asked Rick.

Jim thought for a moment and said, "Well, yes, it is. He handled all of those matters when Gabrielle was alive. She rarely participated with me at all. That is very different." Jim seemed to be appreciating that the balance of power between him and Doug had been significantly altered by Sarah's presence. This was either an opportunity or a looming disaster for his ongoing business relationship with this family.

"Think even harder now," pushed Rick. "What did she ask about in relation to what the other financial company provided . . . what didn't she mention?"

Jim thought for a moment and then said, "Life insurance. She didn't ask about life insurance." He started to laugh, saying, "But nobody ever asks about that."

Rick smiled and laughed. "Fair enough. But what do you want to bet that she didn't ask that of Holistic Financial either?"

"That's likely true," agreed Jim. "And yet, that's where they went first—straight to an insurance review. She probably asked about estate planning and business-succession planning, and the advisors at Holistic went straight to life insurance." Jim smiled.

"They don't even know what this family's values, mission and goals are and they went straight to a tactic," added Rick, taking the opportunity to plant seeds about his new model of client engagement. "Then the family reached out to you, via Sarah with Doug's blessing, to ask, yet again, about estate planning and business-succession planning."

Lights were flickering on across Jim's eyes as he thought more about what happened. "Those knuckleheads missed the whole point of the call. There is some link between the succession of his business and their family estate planning that is causing them to worry. I see what you meant now, Rick. If this was about simple tax planning or life insurance reviews, Doug would have squashed it dead."

"Unless he was interested," clarified Rick.

"But he wasn't interested in that, and she asked again," said Jim. "They weren't listening to the question at all, Rick. Holistic Financial answered the questions they wanted to ask. They didn't listen at all to the clients."

"Their name is very misleading," said Rick, smiling. "They really aren't acting in a very holistic manner."

"Well, let's do this right for these people and really find out what's going on," said Jim "Why don't we try to be the holistic planners?"

Rick was impressed how seemingly ready Jim was for his new model.

"We will answer the questions she asked," said Jim with some resolve. "We will answer their tax questions and whatever other issues they have in their estate and business-succession planning."

Rick decided to corral Jim in a bit. "Well, as I mentioned, Jim, tax will likely not be an issue until the end of our conversation and process with these folks. It's typically a tactical response once a strategic plan has been created. We don't even know what the strategy is yet."

Jim slid back a bit in his chair. "Financial planning, business-succession planning, estate planning . . . those are mostly about tax, right? I mean, otherwise it's pretty simple. Yeah, he's got to move the business to Todd, his son, and maybe get a little cash to the daughter—that's probably where the nexus is between the two types of planning Sarah asked about, right?" asked Jim.

"Well, is there enough in the estate to treat both kids equally?" Rick inquired.

"He once told me that Todd had really helped build the business up and he would get more than his daughter. It wasn't going to be equal, but it would be fair," Jim stated.

"Fair to whom?" asked Rick.

"Todd, his son, of course. He put all the work into the business," said Jim.

"What about the daughter? What does fair mean to her?" asked Rick.

"Kelly," answered Jim. "Her name is Kelly. I always remember her name eventually. Todd's name I get right away because he is also a client."

"Did anybody ask her if she thought getting a smaller inheritance was fair?" pushed Rick.

"That's crazy," Jim responded without hesitation. "It's Doug's business. He can do whatever he wants. Fair doesn't always mean equal. Todd added more value over the years to that business while Kelly studied at university and started her own career. Is that a real question? Are you going to ask that? Because that may piss him off," he fumed.

"The hard questions are the only ones worth asking," Rick stated in response. "He's a big boy, he'll understand the importance of those types of questions. In fact, I bet that is exactly one of the issues he is grappling with—the business assets, his new family and his legacy. Jim, if we don't fiercely ask these questions, who will? After all, what's the harm?" Rick added.

"The harm? The harm? The harm is, we piss him off and he leaves as a client. That's the harm!" blurted Jim.

"He's already got one foot out the door," said Rick.

"No, he doesn't. He won't move his money because of a life insurance review from Holistic. It's embarrassing he went there, but that's it. His returns have been good over the years," said an exasperated Jim.

"Do you have a theory about why he went to that firm in the first place, then?" asked Rick.

"People drip on him all the time. He's probably just using their resources," said Jim.

"Really?" countered Rick. "Is he that kind of a person who would take substantial free resources just because they were offered? With no hope of reciprocity? Is that how you would describe his character?" This had never been Rick's experience with family business owners. They were extremely straight shooters.

Jim thought more and conceded. "No, that's not really his style. Yikes, I am a little worried now. Maybe this relationship is at risk because I didn't offer these services. Do you think that's it, Rick?"

"Maybe not, I don't know enough yet," Rick replied. "We have a great opportunity here to change this conversation and get this done right for the client. That's what you want, right? The best thing for the client?"

"Of course I do," said Jim.

"Would you be prepared to lose this client because they were angry with your advice? If you knew in your heart the advice was in their best interests but was hard for them to hear and accept?" asked Rick.

After only momentary hesitation Jim answered, "Yes."

"Then we will all be on the same page," said Rick. "My hunch is that Holistic not only answered the wrong question but also completely ignored Sarah and spoke only to Doug. My bet is they talked tax, tax and more tax. Insurance to pay tax and ways to avoid probate tax. A corporate reorganization to save tax. A financial plan to structure the income in the most tax-efficient manner. Tax, tax, tax," Rick said in an exasperated tone.

"Ohh . . . ," Jim groaned. "I told you, that's what he loves to talk about most—not paying tax."

"Jim, let me ask a one-word question several times and maybe you will see my point here, okay?" asked Rick.

"Okay," said Jim.

"Why do you want to pay as little tax as possible upon your death?" asked Rick.

"Because I hate paying taxes," Jim said quickly.

"Why?" asked Rick.

"I want that money for other things—things I choose," said Jim.

"Why?" asked Rick.

"In my estate, I suppose I want to make sure I have the most available for my children and my spouse," Jim thought aloud.

"Why?" asked Rick.

"I want my family to be taken care of," Jim said, thinking harder now.

"Why?" asked Rick.

Jim paused. As he reflected, he smiled and said, "I love them and want the best for them."

"Doug will be no different, I am sure," said Rick. He wants to pay as little tax as possible because, at the end of the analysis, he loves his family and wants the best for them. That's his core goal right there. That's what we need to get at and reveal."

Jim crossed his arms and nodded his understanding.

Rick smiled and said, "You know when I asked what would be the harm? I could have asked it a better way. I should have said: Imagine the great peace of mind and comfort you can give these people by helping them get unstuck on tough issues and create solutions for the big dilemmas they face in life. What is the good that can come from that process?"

Jim said nothing as he thought about the question. Then he said quietly, "A lot of good can emerge. But it makes me nervous to ask."

"We grow professionally when we expand beyond our comfort zones, Jim. Do you have access to those reports generated by Holistic?" asked Rick.

"Yes, I have them here, and Doug said I could share them as is appropriate," said Jim, adding, "but so far it's really just an insurance review and suggestions based on the taxes due at death. They dangled the other services, but I'm not sure they have given Doug and Sarah any proposals on them yet."

"Okay," said Rick, "let's take a look and see where we should start. I bet this is a huge opportunity for you, and Holistic Financial, ironically, just dug it out of the ground for you. We shouldn't wait too long though," he cautioned. "We need to move swiftly."

"I will e-mail them to you right now," said Jim.

• • •

Rick returned to his office to clean up his desk and head out for the day. This was his point of no return for planning. He, and the fickle finger of fate caused by excess coffee consumption, had determined Doug Matthews would be the first client to experience his new Abundant Estate approach to planning. And, whether he liked it or not, Jim Fox was going to be the first advisor to receive on-the-job training on how to facilitate the model.

Hopping on the elevator, Rick texted his friend Dave:

Rick:

I have crossed my Rubicon. Using new method with client and advisor

Several minutes later he received a response.

Dave:

Alea iacta est

Rick:

?? I stopped using Latin after law school

Dave:

The die has been cast. You have set down your stake in the ground as an act of rebellion against the old order.

Rick:

You do like drama

Dave:

To some this will be treason. But recall, Caesar prevailed as
a result of his action

Rick:

LOL. My goal is only to advance the client's best interests

Dave:

Stay in control of the table

Rick knew what he meant. This would be different for the clients and everybody who worked with the clients. He needed to be vigilant.

• • •

Later that night at home, Rick sat in front of his laptop and reviewed the various entries he had made during the day. He had already transcribed his notes and reflections from Convergence on the flight home from the conference. He began ordering the concepts and pondering the steps of his own Abundant Estate model.

"I should start to distill the basic steps into a coherent order," he thought to himself. After a great deal of trial and error, he came up with the following:

The Abundant Estate

1. Begin a process of having family meetings to address the various topics for your intergenerational wealth planning.

2. Use a meeting cycle to discover and articulate your shared family values.

3. Use a meeting cycle to create a family mission statement based on the shared family values.

"Okay," Rick laughed, thinking, "it seems really simple, but that's the essence of the first three steps. If these are done right, the engine is primed for some really heavy lifting that will be achieved by step four."

He then spent several hours ordering and recasting the next step of his model. As he was doing so, he thought to himself, "The fourth

step is really less of a step than it is the very core of the strategic
process." It was not a step you move from to another step, never to
return. It was a process that would continuously churn from issue
to issue and generation to generation. It was the powerhouse of the
Abundant Estate—the engine of innovation, growth and sustainability; the creation of a legacy that would last for generations to come.

Eventually, at 1 a.m., exhausted and bleary-eyed from typing,
thinking and revising, Rick had the fourth phase of his planning
model:

Utilize a strategic process:

a. Identify key goals.

b. Set clear objectives to break the big goals down into smaller,
achievable steps.

c. Create strategies to achieve the objectives.

d. Identify and implement specific tactics to execute on the
strategies.

Even though it was a fairly standard strategy model, the purpose
for which it was being deployed was unusual. "It is the central core
of the Abundant Estate," thought Rick. "This is where families and
their advisors take the layers away and start to transition the basic
values they fundamentally share into action. It's where they craft
their stories into a successful, multi-generational narrative. It really
is the expression of their family's very essence. It's an act of creation
from a starting point of clarity and purity."

Finally ready to call it a night, Rick shut down the computer and
walked down the hall, turning off lights as he went. He noticed his
youngest daughter's light was still on. She and her sister had fall-
en asleep together reading a book. They looked too comfortable to
awaken, so Rick turned off the light and smiled in the moonlit room.
His girls were his purpose in life. He doubted it was much different
for anyone else.

Chapter 4
The SMRT Strategic Engine

"See first that the design is wise and just; that ascertained, pursue it resolutely. Do not for one repulse forego the purpose that you resolved to effect."

—William Shakespeare

IN THE DAYS THAT FOLLOWED his conversation with Jim Fox, Rick took advantage of a lull in his schedule to think more about his Abundant Estate model. He realized that creating an estate plan was a challenging process for most people. They didn't really know where to begin but they certainly thought they understood the ending. Everyone thinks that they understand the ending—a quick and tax-efficient distribution of assets to beneficiaries. Full stop. However, the planning story doesn't have to end at death. Rick wanted to change that entire way of thinking because he now believed death was simply another inflection point in the journey of a family's collective wealth. It is a manageable pivot in a strategic planning process based on maintaining continuity between generations.

Understanding estate planning as a *process* rather than a point-in-time activity was essential. Rick's new perspective on wealth-continuity planning eschewed the notion that it was a one-time event between a client and an advisor, usually a lawyer. It is much more than that. It requires engagement, purpose and structure; it needs regular feedback and periodic review; it demands vision, tactics and strategy to achieve a positive and enduring outcome; it is hard work and involves continuous effort and deliberate practice. At its best, it engages multiple generations of the entire family and integrates the multidisciplinary expertise of a robust advisory team.

Rick heard a siren in the street below and instinctively stood to see where the ambulance was headed. At that very moment, his iPhone buzzed with a text from his wife. She was in the neighborhood and wondered if he wanted a coffee. Rick agreed to meet her at the front of the building.

"Let's head to Starbucks," he suggested. "I want to run something past you."

"Ruh-roh," she said, knowing he would appreciate the *Scooby-Doo* reference.

"Ha . . . no, nothing like that. I am trying to articulate an approach to estate planning that is a process, a lifelong process driven by purpose," he said.

"Lifelong? Jeez, you lawyers are always working on schemes to make more money. Good for you," she laughed. "I want a new kitchen."

Rick chuckled and realized her answer was exactly how many people would respond to the notion of estate planning as a lifelong process—with doubt about the need.

"Tell me, what do you think of when you think of estate planning?" he asked Jillian.

"A will," she blithely answered.

"When should you do a will?" he asked.

"Um . . . when you get married, have kids or maybe have a house or lots of assets?" she responded. "I'm in the car now, can't talk. See you in five minutes." They lived about five blocks away from his office.

After they disconnected, Rick began to make his way down to meet Jillian in front of the building lobby. In the elevator, he considered her answer. It was clear that the typical person viewed estate planning as a response to discrete and momentous events in life.

- Just had a child? Do a will to appoint a guardian.
- Just bought a house? Do a will to pass on your property.
- Just moved to a new region? Do a will that reflects the laws of that jurisdiction.
- Your child just got divorced? Review your will to make sure things will pass in an orderly way to future generations.

These major life events are all good motivations for estate planning or, at the very least, for updating a will; however, they are reactions to stimuli in the family. Where is the actual forward "planning" in this approach? Where are the cohesive narrative, goals and values? Where was the process to give shape and structure to the planning? Rick knew that this kind of reactive approach to life events leads to planning conundrums that often can't be solved because the full spectrum of a family's wealth and the broader purpose for inter-generational continuity were never taken into account. As well, underlying issues beyond the immediate trigger events were often allowed to percolate, unmanaged, for too long. In these circumstances, creating a will is akin to placing a time bomb with a long fuse delay into the family.

Rick was standing in the rain at the front of the building when Jillian pulled up in the car. He quickly jumped in and they exchanged hellos and chatted about the kids. As they approached their destination, Rick asked Jillian, "What if I told you that half of all adults in North America don't have a will? Would that surprise you at all?"

"Not really," said Jillian. "Lots of people don't have the money to do estate planning."

"You mean, to pay for the lawyer, or not enough money to bother with a will in the first place?" he asked.

Jillian thought about it for a moment and then said, "Either could be true. Although I know cost shouldn't be a concern, as there are several affordable options. Okay, so the only 'good' reason not to bother is that you don't have enough financial wealth."

"How much is enough?" asked Rick.

She was getting perturbed by his questions. "I don't know, lawyer-man. You tell me how much is enough. Surely there is a number of some sort?" she asked him.

In the interest of self-preservation, Rick stopped talking while his wife navigated between two luxury SUVs in the parking lot. Successfully parked, they alighted from the car and Rick returned to his line of questioning, asking, "Well, I'm not sure there is a specific number but, before I answer that, what do you consider to be our family's wealth?"

She fell silent as they walked along the street to the café. As they entered the door, she said, "Okay, I see where you are going. We don't have a ton of cash. I guess I'm buying the coffees today . . . again. You're such a tightwad."

"With life insurance, I am worth more dead than alive," he smiled.

"Don't tempt me," she quipped. "But we do have friends with connections who can help our daughters meet the right people and enjoy the best opportunities possible in their lives. We have our family's reputation as being honest and trustworthy and my reputation in the arts world," she laughed, purposefully omitting any reputation Rick may enjoy.

"Our social capital," said Rick.

"And we have our skills and abilities and those of the girls and our other family and friends," she thought aloud as they found two seats near the big bay window overlooking the central boulevard.

"Our human capital," said Rick.

"Okay, I get it. Money isn't everything. Is this where you tell me that there was no richer, just poorer?" she joked.

There was no safe answer, so Rick simply laughed as Jillian continued. "There are other sources of family wealth. Most families will have this wealth in some amounts if they really think about it. But come on, Rick, can you pass that stuff on in a will?"

She didn't wait for an answer and, seeing a gap in the line, went up to order while Rick held their seats and continued to ponder. Drinking coffee and pondering were his top skills.

Jillian returned with the drinks and said with a large sigh, "Before I forget, that board I am on meets again tonight. It could be a long meeting."

"Trouble at the mill?" he asked.

"Ugh," she replied. "I'm finding the transition issues that we're grappling with to be very frustrating. Some of the people text me constantly and I'm feeling a little consumed. I find all the relationships and alliances hard to manage."

"Isn't the board working on their succession plan?" he asked.

Jillian was on the board of a local children's arts academy. They were well-known in the community and survived on their reputation; however, for many years they had functioned on the strength and energy of their founders. They were now transitioning to next-generation parents and families for leadership and stewardship. Substantial experience and wisdom had to be transferred from the founders' memories and documented to ensure a smooth and complete transfer of knowledge.

"It has been very frustrating," answered Jillian. "I have been trying to get them thinking about the future—five years, ten years out and even longer. Where are we headed? What are the demographics of our customer base? Can we grow? What are the risks? They aren't used to thinking that way. They just do what they always do and plod along. There is no sense of strategy or long-range goals."

He sipped his coffee and stared at her as she spoke.

"For example," Jillian went on, "every year we give away memberships to children in financial need. But we have no set number we give, no rules about what qualifies as 'need,' no expectations for the gift, no sense of purpose or direction at all. We just hand them out willy-nilly to whoever asks for them," she railed.

He sipped his coffee and stared at her as she spoke.

"What's worse is that nobody knows we do this," she continued. "It's all secret. We could leverage this program in the community and attract fresh blood to apply to play in the orchestra or be on the board. People would probably be aware of us more if we had a strategy for our philanthropy and it could generate some good press. Then, everybody would know the rules."

He sipped his coffee and stared at her as she spoke.

"What they are missing is a strategy. They need to build a strategic approach," she finished.

He sipped his coffee and stared at her as she finished speaking.

"Are you listening to me?" she asked him.

He sipped his coffee and stared at her as she spoke.

Jillian glanced behind her and saw an attractive young college student studying in the corner. "Are you looking at her while I am talking to you?" she laughed.

Sensing imminent mortal danger, Rick snapped out of his trance. "No, no . . . no . . . I was just thinking that you may have reinforced the clarity of my path. Thank you!" he effused.

"What? How does that help you?" she asked, convinced he really was just checking out the girl at the back.

"The problems you just described are the same types of issues that most people have when they are making a will or thinking about estate planning," he explained. "They start from scratch each time and really just respond to issues as they present themselves. There is no overarching sense of narrative, themes or purpose."

"Well, for our board, this means we waste a lot of time arguing over issues that aren't relevant or that have been debated before," she began. "There is no accessible, shared body of knowledge. More often than not, we just don't decide at all. We never ask, 'Why are we doing this?' It's always about the fundraising, or whatever the immediate need is—you know, the activity itself and not the real reason behind it."

"It is a reactive and painful process rather than being a creative and purposeful process," suggested Rick.

"Exactly!" agreed Jillian. "I try to get them to think about values and strategy, but there is a sense that this is the way we have always done it so let's just continue to do it this way. We got here doing it this way. Why rock the boat?"

"People are afraid of change," stated Rick. "Change often means loss of influence or power and it draws people over uncertain terrain. They prefer stasis. It's easier to let things happen than to corral the energy and *make* things happen. In fact, they prefer what's called homeostasis," he offered, finishing his coffee with a slurp.

"Homeo-what?" she laughed as they got up to exit the café.

Rick explained the phenomenon of homeostasis, "Essentially, it describes a circumstance whereby a body exerts energy to maintain its own stability and equilibrium against various external forces."

Jillian scrunched her face up and said, "What?"

"The human body works very hard to maintain a steady state temperature," explained Rick. "It does this whether it is very hot or very cold out. So, depending on the situation, we sweat or shiver as a physical response to external conditions."

"All in the effort to maintain a certain core temperature," finished Jillian.

"Social systems, like a family or family business, are no different," said Rick. "External forces act on them and they burn energy to resist the implications of those forces."

Jillian nodded and said, "All in the effort to maintain a certain core equilibrium in the family. That energy consumption can be substantial. It's a bit like a furnace responding to wide open windows on a cold January day."

This time, Rick scrunched up his face and said, "What?"

"Well, the furnace is trying to maintain the house at a comfortable 72 degrees, but the window is open," said Jillian. "That furnace will burn expensive and precious energy constantly until the window is shut. But how does a furnace know how to shut a window? It's dumb that way; it needs to be smart and interconnected with the causes of the external condition causing the problem in the first place," she thought aloud as they approached Rick's building.

"That's very profound," he said with a grin.

They arrived at the front doors of his office tower. The rain had broken and the sun was starting to show itself in the western sky.

"You said you wanted to run something past me . . . did we miss that?" asked Jillian.

"No, not really," Rick replied. "I wanted to share my idea for what I like to call the Abundant Estate. Your rant about the board simply confirmed that the idea to use a strategic approach was the right one. It gets over a few hurdles with decision-making and communication."

"What model are you using?" she asked him.

He removed his smartphone and showed her the next phase:

Utilize a strategic process:

a. Identify key goals.

b. Set clear objectives to break the big goals down into smaller, achievable steps.

c. Create strategies to achieve the objectives.

d. Identify and implement specific tactics to execute on the strategies.

"You have other steps?" she asked.

"This is the fourth step," he told her. "It's a big one."

"And that step never really ends," she commented as she read the list. "Looks like I will get my new kitchen after all."

Rick laughed and hopped out of the car. As he did so, Jillian asked, "Hey, why do you call it the Abundant Estate?"

Rick replied without hesitation. "Too much of our planning is based on a natural human response to perceived scarcity. We mindlessly consume in the fear that we will lose the opportunity to consume again in the future. In reality, we live in a world of great abundance. Our families are full of abundance. We should be grateful for what we have and invest in perpetuating it. That's the basic core of the name. It's an attempt to invert and broaden how we think of our wealth."

"Optimistic," she said with a wink.

"It's a better way to live, I think," he said with a wave as she drove away.

• • •

Rick returned to his office to continue refining the Abundant Estate model. He decided he wanted a working definition for "strategy." Reaching into his bookshelf, he extracted *The 80/20 Principle: The Secret to Achieving More with Less,* by Richard Koch. He had always liked the definition of strategy Koch used:

> *To be strategic is to concentrate on what is important, on those few objectives that can give us comparative advantage, on what is important to us rather than others; and to plan and execute the resulting plan with determination and steadfastness.*[1]

Family strategy is in part about identifying and reinforcing the shared features that build a powerful strength of kinship. A clear strategic model is also about choosing what *not* to do.[2] In every planning situation, the things that are important to us should never be subordinated to the things that matter least.[3]

Rick had already determined that establishing a set of core family values is an important starting point to underpin the eventual wealth-continuity plan. These shared values are the essence of how the family perceives and defines itself. Purposefully articulating collective family ideals, principles and beliefs is a tremendous opportunity for the family to share very important conversations and ideas as well as experience a common process. Identifying core values establishes a logical launching point into the creation of the family mission statement that then leads into action mode—a truly strategic process for wealth-continuity planning.

The next step was to undertake the difficult and ongoing work of developing the strategy engine itself.

Strategic planning can take many forms. For the foundation of his new model, Rick had decided to include four basic steps that are present in most strategic process models:

1. Identify key goals

2. Set clear objectives to break the big goals down into smaller, achievable steps

3. Create strategies to achieve the objectives

4. Identify and implement specific tactics to execute on the strategies

Rick wanted to organize his thoughts and address the strategic planning process one step at a time. He reflected on his conversation with Jillian and decided this phase deserved a name. Her furnace analogy was excellent. He pondered this more and concluded that a strategic approach rendered a dumb machine into a smart machine. If the family was the machine, using the smart features of a strategic model gives them the tools to diagnose and solve their problems rather than mindlessly burning precious energy to respond to external forces. Strategy leads to adaptability and, as Darwin determined, adaptation is the mother's milk of evolution and survival. This is the recipe for sustainable family wealth.

He decided to flesh out the components before arriving at a name. "Don't put the cart before the horse," he thought to himself. "Seems to be my theme these days."

"The first step in this part of the process is to identify the goals of the plan," he decided.

Rick began typing:

In any wealth-continuity plan, goals might include:
- To maintain family harmony
- To preserve family capital for at least three generations
- To maintain and grow all sources of family wealth

- To promote education as a core family value
- To sustain the XYZ family charity
- To be a communicative family
- To bring purpose to intergenerational planning

At that moment, Auston poked his head in the door to see if Rick wanted a coffee. As always, he nodded in the affirmative and several minutes later Auston reappeared with two Konas. In the interim, Rick had printed off the list.

"Here you go, buddy," said Auston as he placed the coffee on Rick's desk.

"Thanks, Auston," said Rick. "Say, have a look at this list of possible wealth-continuity goals I am suggesting as examples. Do they make sense to you?"

Auston took the list and reviewed it.

"As you know, I am trying to create a better approach to estate planning," said Rick. "The idea is to have clients adopt a process approach to continuity planning for their wealth rather than the typical discrete, transactional and reactive response."

"So these are goals," said Auston. "You are keeping the steps we previously discussed in front of this, right? I mean, goals are something you work towards and which become a measure of the success of a plan . . . right?"

"That's right," said Rick. "Recall from our earlier discussion that I'll take clients through a values-articulation process in order to create a mission statement."

"Right, right. Remind me again, how does the mission statement differ from the strategy piece of goals, objectives and tactics?" asked Auston.

"Maybe we could work with a scenario here to give this some flesh," Rick suggested. "Let's assume we have created some communication skills and now we want to identify core values to create a mission statement."

"Perfect. What are the values you hold dearest in your own life?" asked Auston.

Rick was silent as he considered the question.

"Why don't we each take a moment and create a list?" suggested Auston.

They worked for several minutes and then shared their results. Rick's list included: wisdom, leadership, humor, beauty, loyalty and gratitude. Auston's list was shorter and included: faith, loyalty, grace and courage.

"I see we agree on loyalty," said Auston.

"We likely agree on many others," said Rick. "But time constrained our effort. Ideally," he continued, "I would take much more time and get examples of each of the individual values from the various family members to build a narrative of experience around those values. I don't want them to just list values; I want them to share values they have experienced firsthand. It makes it authentic."

"So, if we were family members and shared loyalty, we would also share stories and examples to illustrate times where we experienced or witnessed loyalty and how it made a positive impression?" asked Auston.

"Yes, and we would also explore situations where loyalty was observed in a negative light. That's important too. Other family members may not highly value loyalty because they experienced something negative around it. We want to understand the bounds of the value so that we appreciate how this family articulates the positive attributes of the value of loyalty," continued Rick.

"That's delicate," said Auston. "I mean, if you didn't value loyalty as much as me, I might perceive that you don't value loyalty at all. You have to carefully manage the discussion around that process. Especially in a family business setting, I bet."

"I agree," said Rick. "This is an area where a family really benefits from a facilitator to help them through the process. That way, they can avoid perception problems and miscommunication. The earlier steps in my process help to build those communication skills. That said, most families will have at least two or three values that are highly ranked and shared. That's the starting point," he finished.

"I suspect the shared values don't change much," mused Auston. "I mean, you may add a value that becomes more important over time, but core values such as honesty and fidelity, for example, don't typically go away; we just come to understand them better over time. So then you take those core values and create a mission statement?" he asked.

"Right," affirmed Rick. "And the mission statement is a very high-level recasting of those core values into a statement of timeless purpose. It's a basic summary of how life for the family will be pursued and realized in the context of their shared core values."

"Huh?" asked Auston.

Rick laughed and continued. "Okay, let's use two of my values: wisdom and gratitude. They are core values. My mission statement is a way to give an action orientation to those values. So, we might say our mission statement is, 'To aspire to live every moment with gratitude for life's abundance and with a passionate desire to learn about ourselves and about the world we inhabit, so that we can each pursue our life's passions, be together as a family and bring happiness to ourselves and our communities.'"

Auston smiled. "Did you just pop that off the top of your head?"

Rick laughed and explained he had been toying with the idea for a while now.

"Okay then, I feel better about how easily you managed that," said Auston, nodding. "The values were identified and processed at the outset of the process, and they feed into some broader outcomes, like being happy and pursuing passion in life."

"Correct," said Rick. "You can see there is a bit of an overlap with the next phase of the Abundant Estate, which is about setting the goals and creating a strategy to achieve those goals. It's an evolving process and there may be refinements and restatements along the way."

"It's not perfectly linear, you mean?" asked Auston.

"Exactly," agreed Rick. "In fact, that's part of the hard work of the process—it isn't linear and doable in a precise timeline with a checklist. But how many of the experiences of life are truly linear?"

"Not many," replied Auston. "There are many forks in every road."

"That type of mission statement is a great backdrop to the strategic process of creating the ongoing planning because any strategic step that works against those values is a non-starter," said Rick.

"And your next phase is the 'How?' to the 'Why?' of the mission statement. It's the blueprint for action and the pathway to success," added Auston, getting up from his chair and collecting his empty coffee cup.

"Yes," stated Rick with enthusiasm. "This family has a great mission it wants to achieve to live their family values from one generation to the next. Now, how do we get there and how do we know if we have been successful? How do we know that we're on the wrong track and need to adjust and recalibrate? What's the road map and how do we make decisions on that journey?"

"I get it now," said Auston. "Keep me posted on this, it's really interesting. I could see integrating it with the goals-based financial planning I do for people."

Auston left the office, and Rick continued to forge ahead. He quickly typed up his mission statement on his laptop before he forgot it altogether. He also updated some of his earlier entries on core values.

After entering the draft mission statement, he leaned back and reflected on his work. "A goal in this setting is really about measuring when there has been incremental success towards achievement of the family's broader mission," he thought to himself. "Attaining goals is what mission fulfillment looks like for a family—achieved goals are a measure of mission success."

He shook his head and thought, "This can get pretty fuzzy. Maybe I should create a family example."

Rick began to reflect on the mission statement he had entered on his computer. Just then his iPhone buzzed. Dave was in the building next door and his meeting was canceled. The two decided to grab a coffee in the food court. Rick quickly updated and printed off his notes from his meeting with Auston.

As Rick headed to the elevator, he saw Jim Fox already waiting there. "Hey, Jim," said Rick as he reached out to shake hands. "I am going for a coffee with a colleague, you want to join us?"

Jim agreed and they shared some light conversation as they took the elevator to the main floor and walked to the food court. Rick spotted Dave in the coffee line and confirmed their order while Jim scouted for a table. Dave and Rick chatted in the line.

"Jim is an advisor I'm working with using the new wealth-continuity model," said Rick.

"Are you working with him or on him?" laughed Dave as the coffees were provided by the barista.

Rick smiled and added, "Frankly, it's been both. I am also evolving. I wanted to show you something I'm working on. I'm helping Jim with a client who badly needs some thoughtful process applied to his family situation."

They joined Jim in the sunny atrium of the food court and made the necessary introductions. Rick then took out the goals sheet he had printed off for Auston, and he shared it with the others.

- To maintain family harmony
- To preserve family capital for at least three generations
- To maintain and grow all sources of family wealth
- To promote education as a core family value
- To sustain the XYZ family charity
- To be a communicative family
- To bring purpose to intergenerational planning

He had also added "happiness, gratitude, learning, loyalty and wisdom" under the heading Core Values. Under the heading Mission Statement, he had added "To aspire to live every moment with gratitude for life's abundance and with a passionate desire to learn about ourselves and about the world we inhabit, so that we can each pursue our life's passions, be together as a family and bring happiness to ourselves and our communities."

"Is this the kind of work we'll do with Doug?" asked Jim.

"I think so, Jim," Rick said and then added, "eventually."

"So you have several core values here, but there would likely be more, I would imagine?" asked Dave.

"Probably," said Rick. "But not necessarily. I mean, the family has to identify the values they are prepared to say they all share. On an individual basis, there will be many more values revealed; on a shared level, however, maybe it'll be just two or three. It will be very idiosyncratic, I would expect."

"And the mission statement is the broader 'why' for this family. Why are they sticking together; why are they in business together; why does it matter; why are they agreeing on process, understanding values, enhancing their communication skills and all the other elements to your model? Really, why does this family matter?" asked Dave.

Rick nodded his agreement. "You can see that a few broad goals have been implicitly inserted, such as pursuing passion in life, family togetherness and fostering happiness."

"So this mission statement could be longer? There could be more elements?" asked Jim.

"Yes," said Rick. "This is a small example just for illustration. So, my question to you two is, what kinds of goals could I suggest to build the strategic engine needed to give life to this mission statement and bring action to these values?"

"I see what you are doing. You are asking the family to describe their vision for the future of their family, their enterprise and their wealth. That's fundamentally a long-term concept," said Dave.

"And then the goals are milestones along the journey. They are markers of success with the mission?" asked Jim.

"Right," said Rick.

The three men then studied the page intently for a moment. As they did so, Liz Stowe walked by with a tea.

"Looks like the fate of humanity is at risk here," she laughed.

Rick and Jim introduced Liz to Dave, and she was invited to sit down and join in. Rick was glad she had accepted. He was certain she had seemed put off to some extent by the manner in which the Gumble meeting had proceeded with Ben Dower.

"We could use some brain power here," laughed Jim.

They explained to Liz what they were doing and she looked at the sheet.

"Well," she started "I would think that a goal should be something you can actually see, feel or touch. I mean, otherwise, how can you tell if a goal is successfully attained or even relevant?"

"Ooh, that's good," said Rick as he wrote it down. "The ability to measure is important."

"So, a possible goal could be 'To be a family that shares aspirations openly and freely,'" said Dave.

"That seems consistent with the broader values of allowing for individual happiness and wanting to preserve family harmony," said Liz. "I mean, the ability to communicate is vital to those considerations. You can't foster gratitude and a desire to seek knowledge if there is disharmony and conflict," said Liz.

"Jim, what do you think about that?" asked Rick.

"I'm still a bit confused," Jim replied. "How does this end up with a will or an estate plan for Doug?"

Dave jumped in. "For any client, the advisor needs to understand where the family is and where they want to be. Neither is easy, Jim. It seems easy because we usually just collect routine statistical information and fill out forms that are essentially pre-printed. Then we apply our professional skill sets and presto, the problem is solved."

"Yes, and I also think we must understand where they came from on the path to this point in time. What is the family story and the narrative of each person in the family? This is precious insight from a planning standpoint," added Rick.

"It sounds like you are really evolving into this process mindset," said Dave with a smile. "The Convergence conference clearly had the desired impact."

The others looked confused, so Rick and Dave took a couple of minutes to explain the conference and its central ethos.

"When I said precious," Rick continued, "I also meant sacred. This information and the space we are creating for the family is sacred area. We are helping them to understand the story of their family wealth and to use that narrative in order to sustain that wealth over many generations. And we need to keep them on track because it's not easy, it's difficult work."

"It's important to get down to the core story and family narrative," added Dave. "It's close to the bone, so trust is essential and we have to respect that this is their story to develop and chronicle, not ours. It's their timetable and their purpose. Our role is to build that vulnerability into a process of growth and decision-making."

"If we did this right," said Liz, "this could go on for many generations. Wow, imagine being the chosen advisor for that legacy of family wealth. That is powerful."

"That level of depth and continuity is rarely achieved, Rick," Dave pointed out. "Estate planning has become very transactional and is priced like a commodity. People seldom have those deep, long-tenured relationships with lawyers anymore."

"Or with any advisors for that matter," added Liz. "And I see it getting worse."

"Why do you say that?" Jim nervously asked.

"Well, look what's happening with predictive technology in all of our professions," she replied. "Artificial intelligence is changing the landscape. Services as a commodity are dead in the water, I feel."

"The frontier will be with holistic, nuanced and broad-spectrum advice," added Dave.

"I can see a future where we have a variety of expertise in different subject areas but the value proposition is in the emotionally intelligent marshaling of those skills," mused Rick.

"The value will be in the ability to bring it all together for the client and be their coach and mentor, to ask tough questions to support real progress," Liz added.

"Then it's up to us to make the process better for everyone, including ourselves," said Rick.

"This is exciting," said Liz. "You know, all advisors face these challenges and the embedded opportunities. Becoming a better advisor in a multidisciplinary world has a lot of practice implications. More thoughtful and purposeful discovery is just one area where massive improvement is possible and sorely needed. My concern, as I reflect on some of my recent client interactions, is, did we ask the right questions in the first place?"

"And," added Rick, "were they telling us the truth from their perspective or from an objective standpoint? Did we fiercely challenge their assumptions and beliefs?"

"Well, how else are we to get this information?" inquired Jim. "If I ask a client who they want as their estate trustee and they say 'Jane Doe,' who am I to challenge that?"

"That's a good question, Jim," said Dave. "You probably have a form you follow when you do information intake from a client. Right?"

"Correct," said Jim. "The forms make sure I collect the important information needed for the file."

"So," Dave continued, "for an estate planning discussion, you have a box on a form that says 'Estate Trustee' and you ask the client who she wants as estate trustee for her will. Is that a fair description?"

Jim nodded in the affirmative.

"Is that the best question to ask? Not the right question, but is it the best question?" continued Dave.

Jim looked befuddled.

"That question assumes that the person knows what it takes to be an estate trustee, what the role looks like and all the plausible scenarios and risks," added Liz, who then looked over to Jim and said, "I hear your confusion, Jim, I use the same forms."

"It also assumes that there is nothing especially unique about this family and its planning goals and aspirations," said Dave. "That is, of course, ridiculous. So, the starting question isn't really who to select as trustee, but for what purposes and outcomes do we select our trustee? What must happen in this situation and what must never occur?" added Dave.

"I see," said Jim. "I shouldn't automatically accept the name until I understand what they are hoping to achieve and then giving some consideration to whether that person will fit the role as it is truly needed."

"To do otherwise is just lazy," said Dave. "It also risks the integrity of the whole plan if the choice is ultimately poor. Moreover, the intended trustee or trustees may need to be prepared for their future role. This strategic process ensures the relationship with the beneficiaries is well-informed and in line with the purpose of the planning."

"In an important way," started Liz, "the values and mission statement help the advisor stay aligned with the deeper needs of the client and their family. The values are where they are and the mission statement is where they would like to take things. So, setting some goals allows us to operationalize their mission."

"Exactly," said Rick. "This is great, guys. Can you think of another goal that would help in our example?"

"Can I just backtrack a bit?" asked Jim. "Where does all this start? How would any advisor or client get going with this approach?"

"Well, once you have family permission to go down this path, one starting point is to interview all of the relevant members of the family and get their description of where the family is, from their perspective, and where they would like to see things go in the future. You would also collect a lot of other statistical-type information. Then, that data will be aggregated and common themes will be highlighted back to the family. You would use that series of interviews to understand individual family members' values at a granular level," said Dave.

"As an advisor, you would look at the values, themes and areas of agreement as building blocks. A facilitator or family enterprise consultant can really help the family in this respect," added Rick. "You could launch into the Abundant Estate model I am building."

"And that would become the eventual basis of the mission statement," said Liz slowly. "Your goal is to help them see what they already want. To bring a sense of consciousness to their aspirations that is then put into motion by the subsequent planning. It's authentic."

Rick stared at Liz and said, "Brilliant—that's it! So, let's consider this in the context of another goal from that list. Let's take a look at 'To be a communicative family.' Is it a goal and how do we approach it?"

There was some silence as they thought about the question.

"Well," mused Jim aloud, "I suppose if we know how they communicate today and how they feel about that communication's effectiveness we have a baseline. They could, individually and then as a group, be asked how that could be improved upon and how you would know it had been improved upon."

"Family meetings could be suggested both to improve communication and to add some decision-making process over the course of the conversation," added Dave.

"Then start forward and make sure you measure by asking at intervals, 'Is our communication more effective? How do we know it has improved? How can we improve it further? What's stopping further improvement?' . . . Wow, this is powerful stuff," said Liz.

Rick smiled and said, "It's the future of all the work we do. Like you said, Liz, I think artificial intelligence and machine learning will take away the repetitive parts of our work."

"The checklists and the inventories that are the usual stock-in-trade will be done automatically," said Liz.

"The human touch of understanding purpose and motivation, getting down to the core values and then building out an operational strategy will be the future in this world," added Rick.

"Shoot," Jim muttered under his breath.

They all laughed and Liz said, "It's not something to worry about, Jim, because it's happening as we speak. All professions and every manner of work are being digitized. The investment world is being challenged by robo-advisors, and accountants have seen much of their bread and butter billing usurped by personal tax software."

"Even the lawyers are seeing it in intelligent algorithms for discovery and will-making," added Dave.

"If there is a checklist or a pattern search element to the work, then there will be an app for that pretty soon," smiled Rick.

"We add value when we realize that's not what people pay us for and we purposefully humanize our service," said Liz.

"So," laughed Rick, "getting back on topic. Is becoming a communicative family a goal, or is it something else?"

"It seems broad and it very much furthers the values suggested in the mission statement. I think we can accept that effective communication is a precursor to furthering gratitude and a capacity for acquiring wisdom because it avoids or minimizes secrets and conflict," added Liz.

"That helps keep the family together and promotes happiness. I think it's measurable, too," added Jim. "I mean, if the family revealed that there was often confusion over planning and expectations, communication changes should reveal less confusion over time. This could be occasionally surveyed after changes are made."

"The surveys themselves are a form of communication," added Dave. "They reveal engagement and a desire to bring everyone into the process."

They all agreed it was capable of being a goal.

Jim quickly added, "I also like the other one on this list: 'To preserve capital for at least three generations.' It seems to fit the values. It's of interest to me professionally as well."

"I agree," said Dave. "There are many sources of capital in a family, so that needs to be discussed and clarified early on. Just as vital, they should create a shared understanding of why capital preservation is so integral to sustaining all of their sources of family wealth."

"The core values here were wisdom and gratitude," said Liz. "To further those themes, they may want to identify the various sources of their family's wealth, like their human capital and social capital, in order to appreciate their unique importance to the family. That's a form of wisdom, and it would certainly make you feel grateful to have it, were it better understood."

"How would they do that?" asked Jim.

Dave jumped in. "Well, they could try to imagine a world where their financial wealth was gone and their intellectual capital, for example, was all that remained. What would the benefits be? What if the intellectual capital didn't exist at all? If the intellectual capital was important, how did we invest in it to preserve it? Was it an accident that it was created?"

"Okay, okay," laughed Jim. "I get it. We need to explore these areas to appreciate the link between their desire for gratitude and wisdom, happiness, togetherness and those sources of wealth."

"As advisors, we also need to know this so we can give the right advice," added Jim.

"I think we all agree on that," said Rick. "Liz, does that goal, if achieved, further the elements of the mission statement?"

Liz thought for a moment and then responded, "It might satisfy and further both, but it doesn't have to because it fulfills one element. I can see there may be many goals. Some will specifically be targeted to achieving gratitude, for example; others will be unique to wisdom. In the case of this goal, I suspect it supports both values to further the broader goals of happiness and togetherness in the family."

"That's a good point," added Dave. "And we don't have to be too slavish to specific technique in this process. It's possible to have paralysis by analysis. Close counts. The key is that advisors and family members be mindful of their values and mission statement as they experience and develop a process of strategic planning."

"I never see this depth of consideration," added Jim. "That likely explains why there is so much litigation. It looks like hard work."

"It is, Jim," said Dave. "But the reward is substantial. The payoff is that your values are preserved and the wealth of the family is purposefully planned in a manner that ensures its continuity between generations. There is considerable research to show that mindful attention to decision-making processes and effective communication are essential to the success of plans."

"I really enjoyed this conversation," added Liz. "If I recall my business school days, there are some more steps you will be adding after setting goals."

"That's right," smiled Rick. "Why don't we agree to meet again and start into the next steps of this process?"

They all decided to meet in two days at the same time and place to move forward with Rick's model.

• • •

Liz, Jim and Rick said their goodbyes to Dave and then shared an elevator ride back to the office. On the ride up, Liz turned to Jim and said, "Yikes, this type of conversation reminds me of Warren Buffett's saying that you can always tell who is swimming naked when the tide goes out."

Laughing, Jim asked, "What do you mean?"

"Well, when bad things happen and catastrophe strikes, you can always see who put the effort in and took care to evaluate the oppor-tunities and risks in their plan. They have swimsuits on—they have a plan that works to shelter and give cover to their vital interests," she elaborated.

"Seems to me this whole process is about getting naked in the first place—no offence," blurted out Jim.

"Go on," said Liz, laughing.

As the door opened to their floor, Jim said, "Well, we can't do any of this planning unless our clients are prepared to share all their deepest goals and desires. You know, to get down to the nitty-gritty."

Liz thought for a few steps and, as they opened the heavy glass door in the lobby, added, "And, as advisors, we have to be prepared to take them there and help them tell their story with purpose. It's really about capturing the richness of their lives and stories."

Rick got to his office first and bid the others farewell. They all agreed they were looking forward to the next meeting.

At his desk, Rick thought about Jim's and Liz's remarks. He liked the idea that this was about peeling back the layers to get to the real core of a family's story and purpose.

"That's why it isn't point-in-time planning but process-over-time planning," he thought. "Continuity planning between generations is not a short technical story but a work of art on a multi-generational scale. It's more like a family opus."

He sat at the computer and added those thoughts to his page on goals. He did his best to capture the discussion with the others and finished with a line that seemed to encompass the general theme of the discussion: "Successful missions are achieved by setting and attaining supporting goals."

• • •

Two days passed, and the calendar alarm on Rick's iPhone buzzed. It was time for his second meeting with Liz, Jim and Dave. He printed off a few copies of his notes and headed down the hall to corral Jim and Liz. Arriving at Liz's office, he observed she was not in.

"Liz away?" he asked her assistant.

"She and Jim Fox had lunch together and she has another appointment with . . . ahh . . . ." She faltered as she checked Liz's calendar.

"Me," said Rick.

"You," she added quickly and laughed.

Rick went to the elevators and started down to the food court below. He suspected that the Abundant Estate had been a catalyst for a good conversation between Liz and Jim over client management process.

In the food court, he saw all three seated at a table in a mildly animated conversation. Rick grabbed a coffee and headed over to join the fray. Dave rolled his eyes with a smile as he shook Rick's hand.

"I totally disagree," said Jim.

"With what?" asked Rick as he sat down.

"Liz feels this is a model for planning that anyone can use. But I think it's really just for the wealthy. I mean, how much would this cost a client to go through all of this in-depth discovery and assessment? The average person can't afford this level of service. Moreover, they won't like it. I am still not at all certain Doug will like this, Rick. He's a tax-oriented guy and this is all fuzzy, touchy-feely stuff," said Jim.

"Do you think it works?" asked Rick of Jim.

"I can see its value for sure," said Jim.

"If you were a client, would you want to be treated with in-depth care, concern and attention by an engaged advisor intent on ensuring your estate plan aligns with your goals and values?" asked Dave.

"Well, ideally, yes . . . but surely," started Jim.

"But what?" asked Liz.

"It's hard work and will take time. It could be expensive. It seems beyond what is usual," sputtered Jim.

"Is it beyond what is required to do a great job?" asked Rick.

Jim sat quietly for a moment and then he said, "No, it's needed to do a great job." He was still struggling to admit that he really liked the idea.

"I know the process seems light and airy, but avoiding conflict and sustaining wealth has value. If you end up in court, I think that's a hard cost," added Dave.

"I see your point. But, surely, only the wealthy could afford this model?" Jim asked.

"Well," said Liz, "for starters, stop calling me Shirley."

They all chuckled as she continued. "As we discussed at lunch, I think we are innovative and smart enough to bring some scale to this so that it comes as close as possible to the full model for almost every client. After reflecting on this over the last two days, it really seems to me to be about relentlessly pursuing the best questions and being thoughtfully curious in listening and responding. How much does that cost? I try to do it already. It's only unusual because we don't do it enough. It's just a purposeful modification of my existing process."

Jim didn't seem totally convinced but was prepared to accept Liz's final point. If he had been better engaged, applied a process and was more authentically connected to Doug, then he may have avoided his current predicament with Holistic Financial.

"Well, in the interest of time, let's move on to the next level. This is where we finished up," Rick said as he distributed the pages. "Successful missions are achieved by setting and attaining supporting goals."

"If I recall, the next step in most strategic models is about objectives being established to work towards the goals," added Liz.

"In the Abundant Estate scenario," said Rick, "we are also describing goals as tangible steps towards mission fulfillment. In that regard, the objectives are about the meaning we pursue in our actions."

"What?" asked Jim with a laugh. "That's a bit cryptic."

They all chuckled at how only a lawyer could take a simple concept and complicate it beyond all comprehension.

"I believe what the counselor is trying to say is that, once key goals are identified, a successful strategic process requires a set of objectives for each goal," said Liz. "Objectives are the next steps taken to attain a goal, and they broadly represent general things you need to accomplish to achieve those goals. Breaking goals down into several concrete, individual objectives will increase the likelihood of success. Attaining objectives means life is given to the goals."

"Well put, Liz. I don't want to torture this too much, but I like the idea of 'meaning' as another way to cast the word 'objective,'" Rick stubbornly persisted. "The purpose of the next step is to bring meaning and life to the goals. It is purposeful now as we go from the broader goal to the more specific ways to achieve that goal. It is something meant or specifically intended."

They all agreed that, to further understanding, "meaning" was a useful way to cast "objectives."

"Let's look at the work we were doing the other day," said Dave. "Can we develop some meaning or objectives for the goal: to preserve family capital for at least three generations?"

"Generally, an objective is a more specific statement as to how that goal will be achieved. It's where we start to give real meaning and effect to the plan in order to eventually arrive at the 'how' in this process," added Rick.

Dave picked up the thought trail. "What if we said, as a possible objective, that we want to identify and grow the various sources of the family's wealth. That gives the family a mark to aim for or some meaning and definition to the goal."

"Okay, so we agree that understanding and detailing the various sources of a family's wealth moves them towards that goal because it helps to know the various sources of wealth with some precision before you can take steps to preserve that wealth?" asked Liz of the group.

They all nodded their agreement.

"What's another objective?" asked Jim.

"Well," began Liz, "we need to know how much financial wealth is required to attain the various goals. The clients could engage a financial planning advisor to ascertain how much money is needed to create a realistic pool of opportunity."

"So," said Dave, "the objective could be reframed as, 'To accumulate sufficient financial capital to achieve the goal mission within, what, ten years?'"

"It's good to have a time or amount on these things," said Liz. "It keeps the ball rolling and sustains engagement."

"How did you arrive at ten years, Dave?" asked Rick.

"Frankly, I just pulled that out of my . . . ," started Dave.

"Okay, okay," laughed Liz. "I get it. You arbitrarily chose a time frame. That's not good enough. There must be a better way. I suppose that's a whole set of conversations for the family to have about how much is enough within a certain time frame, how did we choose that time frame, which assets will be used, can wealth be created with insurance and so on."

"I see," said Jim. "This is not about us telling the clients a suitable time frame and process, this is about them deciding for themselves where they want to be and why at any given point in time."

"Right," added Rick. "It's about how the family takes ownership of their plan and how it gets done. They want it because they created it. It's also a model of good communication that can be used to develop effective future conversations with the advisor. No topic should ever be closed off by the advisor; it's up to the family."

"Okay, so that's a good example of an objective. It has an element of specificity and a time frame for action," added Dave. "As you would add, Rick, it gives meaning to the goal it supports."

"What is the next step?" asked Jim.

"Well," started Liz, "As I recall, the next step in the strategic process is to attach a clear strategy, or strategies, to each stated objective to help make them more achievable. Just as big, overarching goals become more easily attainable by being broken down into multiple objectives, objectives are more easily accomplished by being further subdivided into individual strategies."

"What is the difference between an objective and a strategy?" asked Jim.

Dave interjected, "Well, let's take a simple example. Rick, what is your youngest daughter's loftiest goal?"

Rick laughed and said, "She's still little but she is determined to be Queen of the World."

"You've done a fine job parenting, Rick," said Liz, smiling.

"Okay, well, what is something every queen needs? Or, what do other queens seem to need that makes them a queen?" asked Dave.

"Wealth, a crown, a throne, subjects, power, maybe a nice castle," said Liz.

Dave continued, "So those are her objectives, the things that need to be achieved to attain queenliness. Among other things she needs to get a castle, a throne . . . each of those meaningful things."

Rick added, "Those are her objectives."

"Right, and the strategy is the field plan to attain each objective. So, let's say getting a castle is the objective under consideration. What are some ways to get a castle?"

"Well, you could buy it, inherit it, marry into it, earn it as a reward for effort," added Jim.

"In the old days they would just steal it. I am assuming that's off the board?" laughed Dave.

Rick chuckled, "Yes, please no crime. So we assess each of those possible methods as strategies?"

Dave continued, "Right. You do a SWOT analysis, to assess the strengths, weaknesses, opportunities and threats associated with each possible route to getting a castle. In the end, the family decides which path or paths are viable."

"And if you have done the process of defining your values and creating a mission statement, you may be able to exclude certain strategies right off the top, because that exercise reveals what you will and will not do as a family or member of a family. In your case, Rick, theft is off the board," added Liz.

"Right, knowing what *not* to do is also strategic," added Dave. "So, it is obvious that theft of a castle is not in your family value system. What about marrying into a castle opportunity?"

"I wouldn't like that in my value system," said Rick. "I presume she wouldn't either if that were the sole reason for the marriage."

"So, based on existing facts, that leaves three possible strategies on this list: inherit, buy or earn her way into a castle," Dave summarized.

Rick laughed, "Well, we can also safely eliminate inheriting for right now."

"I see," said Jim. "So that leaves buying and earning into from this list. Now we need tactics that work towards each strategy."

"For instance," he continued, "saving vast amounts of money, having a well-paying career, investing her wealth and planning to reduce her interest and taxes are all tactics. Those are things she can plan for that, when paired with action steps, move towards the objective. In some cases, a multi-strategy plan may be in play to achieve a single objective. For example, she may decide to purchase a castle as one strategy that she will pursue, but she also chooses to earn her way in to one at the same time. To the extent they don't conflict, either strategy may succeed in attaining the stated objective. To keep things simple, though, let's assume the sole strategy adopted is to buy a chosen castle."

"She will need a good down payment, which would require dedicated savings, a good income and probably a good education so she can find a job that supports the income needed. Those can all be done while she is castle shopping or likely much further in advance," added Rick.

"But if she wants it now, then certain tactics and strategies will not work. That's part of the process too—creating strategic timelines and tactical overlays that work across a variety of intervals," added Liz.

"This is a continuous process of taking stock, evaluating position, assessing needs and marshaling resources. It could be hard work," said Dave. "And that's why most people don't do it. It *is* hard work. But it's purposeful and teaches how thoughtful effort and stewardship over all wealth resources is critical."

Liz smiled. "I see that. For example, if you are trying to save up for a castle, you can't be overly frivolous about money and spending on other items."

"Maybe you have to forgo the cottage?" suggested Jim.

"Or the vacations," added Dave. "But, at least you are getting focused on what you really want and taking charge of the acquisition process. I mean, we can let life happen or we can travel through life with purpose."

"There should be other goals too, just in case, you know, Queen of the World doesn't happen," laughed Rick. "I think the other goals could, in many circumstances, be mutually supporting."

"I think that's right, Rick," said Dave. "Multiple goals can be supported by a web of various objectives and tactics. Many will be repeated, so it's good to have a process that reveals the strategic elements to avoid duplication or strategies and tactics that work at cross purposes."

The group discussed the example further. It was simple, but it helped to clarify the different phases in the model. Objectives were general ways to obtain a goal while strategies were plans to achieve the generalized objectives. Tactics were the very last thing, bolted in only after the full process was considered.

"I like this, Rick," added Jim. "I think a lot of people put the cart before the horse and just head straight to tactics. You know, they want to get a tax saving so they confuse doing something with actually getting what they really want in the long term done. In a way, they become penny-wise and pound-foolish by failing to do the hard work at the front end, of thinking ahead with their values and mission in mind."

"There are no shortcuts to purposeful continuity planning and there is an order of operations, Jim," said Rick. "Sometimes it may feel a bit tedious but it's worth it in the end to make decisions that start with values, mission and goals, and finish with strategies and tactics."

"Your daughter's global domination plans are cute, Rick," said Liz, smiling. "But let's tie this in to our earlier discussion. The goal was to create family wealth that will last three generations, and one objective was to grow the various sources of family wealth. What's the strategy there? What strategies will achieve that objective?"

As the others discussed Liz's questions, Rick reflected on the family whose goal was to create wealth that would last for one hundred years. He knew that research and the anecdotal experiences of peers in relation to successful intergenerational transitions revealed clear answers. Families that were successful in this goal created objectives that included:

- Having ways to manage conflicts
- Being able to talk to one another as a family
- Getting the right help and advice
- Having a process to stay on track
- Knowing what they want and don't want
- Having a growth mentality about family wealth
- Understanding their family's true wealth

Rick wrote down this list and then interrupted the banter of his colleagues, saying, "I was thinking while you guys were babbling, and here are a couple of strategies. First, what about 'Build financial knowledge of all family members' or 'Provide ongoing opportunities for leadership for family members.'"

The others liked those two suggestions and added several of their own that had emerged from their conversation.

Dave suggested, "Nurture and grow healthy relationships among the family members" as a possible strategy.

Liz chimed in with, "How about 'Create opportunities for personal growth for family members and invest in and develop the family's culture?'"

They all agreed they had compiled a useful strategy list that would generate a variety of tactics.

As Rick reflected on the two lists created in this meeting, he observed that objectives were broad and more about knowing, reflecting, comparing and assessing. By contrast, the strategies tended to be action-oriented. The strategies are the plans of action, like a recipe from a cookbook. They require tactics to come to life.

"Can we just take a brief bio and e-mail check-in break?" asked Jim, already three steps away from the table heading towards the washroom.

They all agreed to stretch their legs. Rick had his notepad and decided to prepare a brief summary. He was getting overwhelmed by the concepts in play.

He wrote:

Goal: To create family wealth that will last three generations
Objective: To sustain and grow the various sources of family wealth
Strategy 1: To nurture and grow healthy relationships among family members
Strategy 2: To invest in and develop the family's culture
Strategy 3: To create opportunities for personal growth
Strategy 4: To provide leadership opportunities in the family

Strategy 5: To build financial knowledge of all family members

Strategy 6: To identify and describe the various sources of family wealth

After everyone returned, Rick shared the summary he had created. They all agreed it was a starting place and would, in real life, need refinement and discussion.

"All right," said Rick, "I took a few editorial liberties there, but now that we have several possible strategies to preserve wealth for three generations, let's consider tactics."

"Tactics are the things we need to actually 'do' to achieve success in a strategy," added Dave.

"Broadly speaking," said Liz, "in estate planning, a tactic may include the implementation of a multi-generational trust with specified features or another element in an estate plan like a will and power of attorney. It could mean purchasing life insurance. It might also include introducing tax structures, such as the creation of a holding company."

The group agreed that in the case of the client with the goal of sustaining family wealth for at least three generations or one hundred years, one of their first strategies would be to provide opportunities for leadership in the family.

"So, what tactics help us out?" asked Rick.

"Well," said Liz, "most families should consider a series of regular meetings to do all this work. Organizing, planning and carrying out those types of events requires leadership and organizational skills. The nice thing about that is it can be shared by many people in the family and the leadership role can be alternated to generate opportunities for anyone in the family."

"Many wealthy families have formal governance bodies to help with their decision-making," added Rick. "Having a formal process to groom family members to successfully chair and lead these bodies is an excellent leadership development opportunity."

Jim jumped in and said, "I suppose in more complex situations where there is a family office or a family foundation, those entities need leadership as well."

"In less complex situations, it could be as simple as taking charge of arranging and making sure that regular meetings happen at the kitchen table to discuss specific topics like estate planning and investment awareness. Maybe arranging to have an investment advisor come to speak about tactics to reduce tax in investing," added Dave.

"The family should take some time to make sure they understand what they mean by 'leadership' as well," added Rick. "For example, I am somewhat of an introvert, yet many people will see me as very extroverted. However, I assume leadership in very specific circumstances. That difference in perception can lead to miscommunication."

Liz nodded. "That's a good point, Rick. We don't want families to assume that leaders are simply the loudest or the brashest. The opportunities that are created should accommodate as many personal styles as possible that exist in the family. So that no one is excluded."

"We know that because that would be inconsistent with their mission statement of promoting harmony and personal happiness," said Jim. "Wow, this really is a powerful way to do things. You end up thinking about what you are doing because you are so sensitive to the 'why.'"

"Right, so any drafting, organizing, setting up or implementation of anything tactical would need to be sensitive to those foundational principles," finished Dave.

"Okay," said Rick, looking at his watch. "We are over time here, I am sure. We should meet regularly as a group to discuss this model. I really appreciate your insights."

"This could be the start of a nice multidisciplinary mastermind team, Rick," added Dave.

They all parted with the promise of meeting regularly to build a better holistic process for their clients.

• • •

Rick returned to his office and sat in the chair looking out over the city. He leaned back and pondered the model he'd started to build. He thought that perhaps the most important benefit of a strategic estate-continuity process is that it results in a purposeful estate plan.

The tactics that are eventually chosen are intended to move in harmony, to achieve specific strategies, which in turn accomplish major objectives—all aligned and working together towards a desired goal or set of goals. This goal is the driving force for the entire plan, infused as it is with the core values of the family that are captured in the very first step, articulating the family mission statement.

As he reflected on his scribblings and notes, Rick was drawn to several key words he had circled at various points. He took the highlighted words and phrases from each step of the strategic process and rewrote them in corresponding columns:

Goals   Success in the achievement of the mission
Objectives   Meaning is brought to goals
Strategies   Recipe for action
Tactics   Things that will be done to execute on the strategy

"Hmm," he thought as he looked at the second column. "SMRT. That's really clever—this process is a smart process. That's what I can call it going forward." He smiled to himself as he realized some people would ask how smart the process can be when it is misspelled.

"There's always one left-brain crank in the crowd," he thought. The "A" that is unstated but always present is the adaptability needed and created by this process. A family that makes use of the SMRT model must be willing to adapt from their old ways of approaching wealth-continuity planning. They can also look forward to becoming more adaptive as the process is refined within their experience.

He clipped his Abundant Estate piece onto a new page and added the new acronym:

The Abundant Estate

1. Begin a process of having family meetings to address the various topics for your intergenerational wealth planning.

2. Use a meeting cycle to discover and articulate your shared family values.

3. Use a meeting cycle to create a family mission statement based on the shared family values.

4. Utilize a SMRT strategic process:

   a. **S**uccess in the achievement of the mission is made possible by identifying key personal and family goals.

   b. **M**eaning is brought to goals by setting clear objectives to break the big goals down into smaller, achievable steps.

   c. **R**ecipes for action are established when strategies are created to achieve the objectives.

   d. **T**hings that will be done to execute on the strategy are tactics.

Rick leaned back in his desk chair and sighed as he thought to himself, "This is the model I will use going forward with families. No more order taking. From this point forward I am engaged as a Sherpa in their journey, to help them find their unique path to successful wealth transition between generations."

Chapter 5
The Abundant Estate in Action

"In the long history of humankind (and animal kind, too) those who learned to collaborate and improvise most effectively have prevailed."

— *Charles Darwin*

SINCE THEIR INITIAL MEETING, Rick had obtained more information from Jim Fox about Doug Matthews's situation. Jim had gone back and asked his client a few questions and it was decided that a face-to-face meeting would be useful for all the parties.

The facts were still incomplete, but what Rick now knew about Doug was all too familiar. He had seen similar situations many times over the years.

Matthews had started working in his father's manufacturing business about twenty-five years earlier. It had grown considerably from its very modest roots since he had taken it over when his father passed away very unexpectedly from a heart attack at age fifty. His lawyer, Ross Packer, was Doug's friend from university. Packer and Doug were about the same age, Jim was a little younger; they were generational contemporaries and shared many common perspectives and experiences.

Matthews's first wife was Gabrielle. She was Doug's rock through the lean years of the business after his father's death. Their family was just starting to enjoy a comfortable life as the business changed its market and began to grow when she was felled by cancer. Her death was a terrible blow to the family and the two children suffered. Doug had always invested his time in the business while Gabrielle tended to the family. Her loss was also deeply felt in the community, where she had been a leader and a seemingly unstoppable local force for good.

Gabrielle died soon after her diagnosis. At the time, neither Doug nor Gabrielle had a will. Their joint accounts passed easily to Doug and the house title was changed without much effort. He had always owned all the company shares, so it was a thankfully simple transition at a rather dreadful time.

Rick realized this simple transition had probably fostered a lackadaisical approach to Doug's continuity planning. There had been minimal planning before Gabrielle died and things transitioned very easily. There were no negative consequences from the nominal estate planning and this acted as positive reinforcement for continued inaction.

Several years after Gabrielle's death, Doug met Sarah at a trade conference in Las Vegas. She was there for another event and they met sitting beside one another at a Céline Dion concert. He stepped on her toe while trying to exit discreetly between numbers. They courted for a few months online and she was soon a regular fixture in his life. At the age of sixty, Doug had discovered a new zest for life and enjoyed the time he spent with his new companion. At forty-three, Sarah was a divorcée with a twenty-year-old son, Arthur.

Todd Matthews was Doug's son. He was the oldest child and had been in the business from a very young age. He didn't complete high school and had never worked anywhere else but Doug's operation, ScrapCo. He was a hard worker and his life revolved around the business. Todd and Doug spent long hours every day at the office solving service issues and working with clients. Todd was a model employee, knew every aspect of the business and was well-respected by the other employees. However, Doug occasionally expressed frustration that Todd was disinterested in human resources and strategic thinking. Todd was unmarried but had a serious new girlfriend, Wanda.

Kelly, Doug's daughter, lived in Hawaii, where she was a researcher with an organic food grower. She had married a local Hawaiian and they had two children. Kelly had been estranged from her father for many years. Rick learned they had suffered relationship issues for some time, in part because Kelly had always been disgusted by the polluting she thought her dad's business caused.

As Rick reflected on the Matthews' family story, he was struck by the commonness of the facts: second marriage, family business with one child in and one child out, a seemingly numbers-oriented entrepreneur and the usual travails and joys of life. "These situations are everyday experiences for most advisors," he thought to himself. He was then saddened to realize how many of these milieus he had seen in the past and had failed to approach with ferocious curiosity and purpose. This time it would be different. He was about to use his Abundant Estate model on this engagement. He was preparing to approach a common-fact scenario with an uncommon planning model.

Today was the initial meeting. Rick phoned Jim to confirm the start time. "Are we still good for ten o'clock?" Rick asked.

"Yup, he texted that he is parking the car now," said Jim.

"Excellent. Is Sarah with him?" asked Rick.

"I hope so, but I may have dropped the ball on that, Rick. I was originally communicating only with him and I didn't confirm that they should both be attending today. I am not sure if Doug will be certain to bring her along."

"Okay then," said Rick, "I will head up to the conference room when he gets here."

Rick was very discouraged that Sarah may be absent. She was a stakeholder in Doug's life and her curious outreach had started this whole ball rolling. He pondered the best approach to ensure she was not excluded from this entire process even if she missed the meeting today. Rick was quite certain that if Jim had set up the meeting today, he would have insisted Sarah attend.

A text signaled that Doug had arrived. Rick made his way up to reception on the thirtieth floor, where an anxious Jim met him at the security door and admitted him through to the conference room. There he met Doug Matthews and, surprisingly, Sarah Spencer Matthews.

"Well, well, well," thought Rick to himself, "I already like Sarah. This is going to play out much differently than some people may have expected."

Rick observed that Jim seemed visibly unsettled sitting across from Sarah. He tried to break the ice with some humor, but it was apparent that Jim was not at ease. Rick guessed that he was surprised she had shown up at all and that something had changed in his relationship dynamic with Doug. Despite Jim's substantial progress with Rick's new approach to planning, his old ways and apprehensions had automatically surfaced in a moment of uncertainty. For the first time ever with this client, Jim may have been on some unsure footing. This was likely to be a turning point for everyone at the table.

"Well, let's get started," said Doug as he checked his watch. "I have a meeting at 11:15 and I can't be late."

"No problem," Jim said obsequiously. "We can do this in one hour . . . right, Rick?"

After a painful few seconds of silence, Rick answered, "Doug, we can't possibly get anything meaningful done in one hour. I will just take this time to talk about what I do and why it's important, and maybe discover what you hope to achieve from the process. We can arrange a follow-up meeting if you decide that it's important enough to you to give it some additional time. I think you will want to do that."

Doug turned a little red. It matched Jim's face. However, Sarah was visibly pleased to hear what Rick had to say and she chimed in almost immediately.

"Oh my goodness," she said, putting her hand on Doug's arm, "I am so relieved. We need to talk about these issues. They are so important to our lives and our children. Doug, I have been at you for some time to look at the existing plan and make sure everybody is aware of it and understands what we want to do for our family when we die. This is a great chance to flesh it all out."

That let the temperature go down, and was a great segue for Rick.

"Frankly, this is my preferred way to start: Review the parameters and make sure that everyone is on board for where this might go. We are in a process of framing how we will interact with one another going forward. This is not a business meeting after all. This is about your family and your life's passions. The other thing I would like to comment on is your statement, Sarah, that you wanted to do things 'for' your family. I love that you said it that way. That is what purposeful planning means. In my experience, I have observed that financial wealth is about investing in the people, causes or things we love most. It sounds like you agree," added Rick.

"That's what I want us to accomplish; I couldn't have said it better. In fact, I am not sure I have ever heard a lawyer say it that way at all," added Sarah.

"Recovering lawyer," said Rick with a wink and a laugh. "Well, let me walk you through the thought process. I think you will find it's different from how you usually approach estate and tax planning—I feel it's more accurate to call it wealth-continuity planning," said Rick as he began to share his new model with the clients. "My process is about understanding the true values and wealth your family possesses and investing in those values and wealth sources in a strategic and purposeful manner. This is the model I am proposing."

Rick handed out copies of *The Abundant Estate* and then began to read it aloud:

The Abundant Estate

1. Begin a process of having family meetings to address the various topics for your intergenerational wealth planning.

2. Use a meeting cycle to discover and articulate your shared family values.

3. Use a meeting cycle to create a family mission statement based on the shared family values.

4. Utilize a SMRT strategic process:

   a. **S**uccess in the achievement of the mission is made possible by identifying key personal and family goals.

   b. **M**eaning is brought to goals by setting clear objectives to break the big goals down into smaller, achievable steps.

   c. **R**ecipes for action are established when strategies are created to achieve the objectives.

   d. **T**hings that will be done to execute on the strategy are tactics.

He started into his piece on the goals that clients might have in planning when Doug, clearly reading ahead, interjected, "Wow, this looks like a long slog and a lot of work for our family."

Rick responded slowly, "Most things in life that have enduring value require effort and sacrifice. Let me ask: When you buy something or hire someone, why do you do that? How do you make that choice?"

Sarah commented, "Well, we want something specific done; some insight added. And we want value for what we pay."

"I would agree," added Doug.

Jim also nodded his agreement and added, "In our world, fees and charges are becoming increasingly transparent. Clients are always seeking full value for what they pay. Some of the value we add includes advisory services like Rick offers. That added value distinguishes me from our other competitors in the field. I do more than simply provide investment advice—I provide wealth management guidance."

"It's really important to us to have that added breadth of professionalism and wisdom," Sarah said. "Life seems so complex sometimes and we don't always know where to turn. That's why I reached out after we met the Holistic Financial people. I felt they were using a goals-based discussion just to make us move over as clients. When I asked the Holistic advisor about her actual wealth management process, she had no answer. It just seemed very self-serving and manipulative of our emotions."

Doug interjected. "Rick, in preparation for this meeting, Jim asked a whole pile of personal questions."

Rick glanced at Jim and thought he saw a blood vessel bursting on his left temple.

"And?" asked Rick with a smile, anticipating what was coming.

"And, I have never been asked those questions before. Jim has never asked those questions before," Doug finished.

"Well, it was just that . . . ," sputtered Jim.

"No, no," said a smiling Sarah with her hand raised. "It's amazing. We want those questions asked. It gives us a great deal of comfort to think we might be able to put some of these concerns out on the table with people we trust."

As everyone briefly reflected to take stock of that important comment, Rick observed that Jim's face had regained its usual color. He decided to move ahead with the questions.

"Let's talk about value a bit more, he said. "Doug, what is the 'value' a lawyer provides in a will planning process?"

"Well, I want the will done right so that it works and achieves what we wanted for our planning," Doug responded, gesturing to Sarah.

"Shouldn't every will work?" asked Jim.

"I think that is a great question. We expect the will to work. I expect the accounting advice to work. I understand where this is headed, Rick," added Doug. "You are suggesting that a functional estate document is table stakes. That is the bare minimum—that is the commodity."

"Exactly," said Rick. "So, where is the value that gets added to that will?"

"Experience and training? Maybe being a specialist in the field? Added qualifications and skills?" Sarah suggested.

"Would you go to Jim for heart surgery? Or if your child needed cancer treatment?" asked Rick with a smile.

They all laughed and agreed that no one in the room should be doing any heart surgery.

"So expertise is where some of the value comes from," said Doug.

"That's what we are paying for, that difference between the commodity of the output and the process and wisdom that went into it from the very beginning," said Sarah.

"What do you mean by wisdom?" asked Jim.

"Well, knowledge is knowing whether a tomato is a fruit or a vegetable," said Rick.

Sarah smiled and completed the statement, "But wisdom is knowing whether to put it in a fruit salad or a tossed salad."

"I think so," said Rick. "And I really like the word you used earlier, Sarah: estate planning is a 'process,' not an event. Tell me, what prompted the last will you did? What facts or life events triggered your desire to update the plan you had or create a new plan altogether?"

"We were going on our honeymoon to Hawaii and to visit my family in Maui. Kelly, my daughter, couldn't attend the wedding and the business was crazy busy when we tied the knot. It was pretty chaotic. We left for Hawaii six weeks later for a month. We called the lawyer just before we were leaving, and she did the wills almost on the runway at the airport," laughed Doug.

"I bet she had been at you to do a will after you were married because that event had some consequences?" Rick asked.

"She wanted us to do it before the wedding but, as Doug mentioned, it got a little hectic," added Sarah.

"Excellent, she is a great advisor. Clients get busy and stuff happens. She was proactive and kept you on your toes," Rick added.

"Michelle has been my business lawyer for years, together with Ross. She is his associate. I trust her with all my business matters. They have never steered us wrong," added Doug.

Sarah reached into her bag and removed their wills and passed them to Rick while Doug spoke.

"Thank you for sharing these documents," Rick said as he took the wills. "I would love to take a look at those to see what you have in place. I will look at them later, though. My hunch is, those wills were emergency plugs just in case the plane went down somewhere over the Pacific?"

"Yup," said Doug, "that was about it. I called Ross, and he had Michelle whip them up that afternoon."

"It's refreshing to see that you have a great relationship with your lawyers and that they service you very well. Now, tell me, have there been discussions since to modify your wills or bring them up to date?" asked Rick.

"Well, nothing has changed since those wills," responded Doug. "They are good enough."

"Good enough," thought Rick to himself. "Therein rests the problem." The wills were done quickly with little or no deep consultation and the clients simply deemed them good enough; even worse, they had not been updated or even reviewed in the meantime. Rick believed that successful wealth continuity was about managing the changes in our strategic life plan. He found it difficult to believe that nothing had changed in the intervening years for this family.

"Well, now I have some concerns for your planning," added Rick. "I am wondering how many things in your life you accept when they are simply 'good enough.' I mean, really, Mr. Matthews, good enough for what? Good enough to do what? Good enough for whom? You or your family? You seem like a gentleman who accepts only the best from his life," Rick gestured to Sarah who nudged Doug with a friendly elbow.

"Yeah, just good enough?" she said with mock anger.

Doug paused for a moment, then laughed and said, "Okay, okay, I should be more concerned about this stuff. Sarah is, and that's why we are here today."

Rick shot Jim a quick look after Doug's comment. Raising his eyebrow, Jim acknowledged that he'd heard the answer very clearly.

Doug continued. "I suppose I am, too. However, when we did our wills, my lawyers assured me they were fine for a while and that the estate taxes that will be due are low and the plan is simple and efficient."

Rick visibly cringed into his chair. He then took a deep breath, leaned in to the clients and asked, "Doug, tell me, is your family simple and efficient? Do you view your family as merely tax deductions or income-splitting opportunities?"

Once again, Jim looked like he'd had a stroke. Doug stared back at Rick, looked at Sarah, sighed, and then said, "I'd like to think it's simple, but . . . no. It's pretty complicated, really."

"It's modern," said Sarah, squeezing Doug's arm again.

"That it is, Doug. It is modern and, I think I can add, based on what Jim has told me, not all that complicated if we look at it the right way. So let me ask another question . . . back to 'good enough.' When you say that, good enough, what do you mean? Good enough for whom?" asked Rick, sensing the wall was down and the real work was about to get started.

"Good enough for us," he said, looking at Sarah.

"And the children," added Sarah.

"So, let's get down to brass tacks and identify who we really plan for in your case, okay?" asked Rick.

"Rick, it's everybody: Sarah, Kelly and the kids, Todd and now Arthur, Sarah's son, is very much part of my planning as well," added Doug.

Rick quickly glanced over at Sarah and noted that she seemed a little surprised by this comment.

"So, in the years you have been together, a lot has changed. Your family situation has evolved and you have new relationships that didn't really exist when those wills were drafted. I would bet that they don't at all reflect your emotions and needs right now," said Rick.

"You are right," said a thoughtful Doug. "I think there will be gaps."

"If I may, let me ask you another question," said Rick.

"Please, go ahead," added Sarah.

Noticing her interest, Rick turned directly to Sarah and asked, "Sarah, as you sit here today, what is the absolute worst thing that could happen as a result of your estate planning? What kinds of things would fill you with regret today if you knew you could have taken steps to avoid them and didn't for whatever reason?"

As Sarah paused to contemplate, Rick glanced at Doug, who interjected, "Can I add one thing from my perspective?"

Sarah nodded her approval and Doug continued, "I have never been asked that question before, but for the longest time I have really had a fear about the legacy I leave to my children. I was always an entrepreneur. It is the gift I have, if I have any at all to give to my family. I think it's a gift because it brought us some financial security and the ability to do things and have experiences in life. My greatest fear is that this financial bounty will destroy the 'get up and go' of my children and grandchildren. You know what I mean? I am concerned our financial wealth will cause them to lose any desire to better themselves or to be curious or to take risks and be entrepreneurial in their lives. I fear they will wait for the world to come to them rather than going out and meeting life head-on."

Sarah let out an audible gasp and said, "Doug, I couldn't have said it better. With respect to Arthur and myself, our life was challenging for its own reasons, but I feel we endured because we valued things like education and togetherness. I am really worried that money will change that for our grandchildren. I would be filled with regret if I knew my grandchildren were lazy, entitled and without purpose in life. What a horrible way to experience life. I would blame myself for that if it happened because that's learned behavior."

Doug laughed aloud and said, "Well, that's a side of you I have never seen before."

"And?" she smiled.

"I like it, and I totally agree," he replied. "To specifically answer your question, Rick, I would be filled with regret to know that my legacy to my grandchildren ruined their lives. I would be fearful it would damage their ability to have meaningful relationships with spouses, one another and the work they choose to do."

"You want your legacy to lift them up in life, not weigh them down," added Jim thoughtfully.

There was a reflective silence in the room. Rick saw he was running out of time, but so far the meeting had been a great success. He made some final comments to wrap things up.

"It appears to me that we have some significant agreement on what cannot be allowed to happen with your family wealth," Rick began. "That's about identifying shared values and goals and making them the basis of your planning. Doug and Sarah, this has been fantastic. Look, we had limited time to explore a big topic. We didn't even discuss ScrapCo. Coming in to this meeting, you didn't know me from Adam and so we took some time to make sure there was a bit of comfort between us, and you have been so forthcoming. I think there is some trust here about what we can add. I am going to take these wills and review them, but my hunch is, I don't even need to do that because new ones are likely necessary. We are starting to draw on a blank canvas now. But I am going to leave you with a couple of things for our next meeting. A couple of things I want you to think about . . . okay?" he asked.

"Okay," said Sarah.

"Sounds good," added Doug.

"Perfect," said Rick. "First, we ran out of time before I could fully explain my concerns for your estate plan, so let's finish on that note. I can tell you that a lot of that concern has dissipated because I think we are all on the same page now. At least we agree that this planning process is about more than taxes and efficiency. It's about you and your family. What we also know is that 'family' means something really different to you both than it did when you last did your wills. That said," he continued, "I want you to think about this statement: I plan for my family. It's a pretty loaded statement for only five words. Ask yourselves what you understand planning to mean and what you understand by 'my family.' And, most importantly, think about the little word that hooks it all together, 'for,' . . . ask yourself why that word could possibly be so important to this phrase."

They agreed to discuss the phrase with one another in advance of the next meeting.

Rick looked at Jim and said, "You are the critical linchpin at the table here today, Jim. You are a friend, an advisor, a confidant and, in some respects, a *consigliere* for this family."

Doug hummed a familiar bit of the theme song from *The Godfather* and everyone laughed.

"I hate to use that exact term sometimes but everyone understands the reference. Jim, you are a trusted advisor to this family," said Rick, sweeping his hand to include Sarah and Doug. "You are a person who can connect the dots for the lawyers, accountants and other advisors. You see them most often as part of your regular account review process. You see them a couple of times a year or more. It's a great opportunity to adopt a broader spectrum of conversation and add great value. It's an opportunity to look forward and plan. Really, it's a perch of honor."

"I never really thought of it quite like that," Jim candidly added.

"I want to start in on the Abundant Estate strategic model for your planning, which all stems from the core reasons you do the planning in the first place," said Rick. "Jim has been a big part of our multidisciplinary team that meets to discuss this model."

Sarah nodded her approval, which was duly noted by Jim.

The meeting concluded and everybody seemed content that something important had been achieved. The advisors and clients were on the same page for process. All that needed to be done was to reveal the core story of their new family to put on that page.

After walking Doug and Sarah to the elevator, Jim came back and said, "Man, I wasn't sure where you were going for a minute there. Are all your meetings like that?"

"Like what?" asked Rick.

"Intense like that," said Jim. "Very personal and on the edge of the nasty stuff."

"Well, yes," agreed Rick. "Since I got back from San Diego, I am being more fierce and deliberate about my approach and expectations, and you see the model evolving. I have used elements of the Abundant Estate in different files, but these are the first clients to get the full offering. We can't ignore the emotional aspect of decision-making. People aren't really all that rational sometimes; they can be very emotion-driven. But, the emotions are there, they are real and they need to be laid bare so they can be managed. Later, at a will reading, is a terrible spot for major issues to be exposed. People will fight for sure then. This is one of my pet peeves—the timidity of advisors to dig in and get dirty with their client's personal situation. That's where people often need the most assistance getting unstuck," Rick lamented.

"I was a little surprised that Doug let Sarah carry the conversation so much," Jim noted.

"It's powerful intelligence, Jim," said Rick. "We know, just by observing his responses and her strong engagement, where the nudge points are."

"Nudge points?" asked Jim.

"Sorry, that's just a phrase I use," Rick explained. "I read a fantastic book called *Nudge*[1] that deals with human behavior and decision-making. The essence of the book is that people can be gently nudged towards better decisions and paths. Never to do harm, but to bring people through or around a barrier that prevents them from taking affirmative steps that will better their lives. Doug displayed some strong emotions today. He really loves his wife and family. He just needs to be guided gently to a process that lets him say that . . . at least in his actions. He wants permission to be authentic."

"I was a little surprised he admitted to being fearful," Jim added thoughtfully. "He's always been such a tough and no-nonsense type of guy."

"It was so revealing," said Rick. "Fear is a powerful emotion and it generates many responses. We must be very thoughtful and respectful of that sacred information."

"Is it right to manipulate his decisions and choices? Aren't those his to make?" asked a concerned Jim.

"Absolutely," said Rick. "The whole idea is to let him actually take ownership and commit to making decisions. But, frankly, how does he even know what is good for him from a planning standpoint? What he does know, innately, is that he loves his family. And we know that his family now has new meaning to him—that's sacred information too. We can explore that to divine just how much it means, and why. This allows us to discuss strategic solutions that will seem obvious when they are raised. We can eliminate objectives and strategies by taking away the false choices. There can sometimes be too much selection in a planning store."

"I agree," said Jim. "Having to make choices can be paralyzing. Yet, when choice is removed from us, we feel limited and restricted. Clients want to know all the options, but there are so many. How do we filter the selections?"

"In some cases," said Rick, "it's a framing issue and simple to resolve."

"What do you mean?" asked Jim.

"Well, you often complain the elevators in this building are too slow, right?" asked Rick.

"They are too slow," Jim confirmed. "It bugs me. We pay all that rent. . . ."

"How could they fix that?" asked Rick.

"Put in new elevators, I suppose," suggested Jim.

"And that hasn't happened because?" asked Rick.

"Usually the answer is expense. It costs a lot of money," answered Jim.

"Now, what if we reframed the original complaint in a different way?" proposed Rick. "What bothers you about waiting? Is it the time lost or the fact that you just stand there and stare at the unopened doors?"

"I'm sure the time is negligible," answered Jim. "It just seems like a long time because you're just standing there waiting."

"How could that be remedied?" asked Rick.

"Distract me, I suppose," said Jim. "Maybe with a TV or something that takes my mind off what's really happening. Like they do at amusement parks with lines that zigzag or in a doctor's office with interior waiting rooms. I see what you are getting at. A couple of television sets in the elevator may distract me enough that I don't notice the ride duration."

"And at much less expense. It's just an example to stop your constant complaining," laughed Rick.

"I see the point," said Jim. "Problems often can be reframed in a manner that generates an easier-to-implement solution. This helps people get unstuck. Your strategic approach should help with that."

"I hope so. The Abundant Estate that we discussed with Dave and Liz is a great start," offered Rick. "We need to help clients build some structure and process around their choices and decision-making. This helps to weed out the biases we all have and really challenge the reasons for planning to ensure it is aligned with key goals."

"You know," started Jim. "I have always sensed that clients are intimidated and challenged when they go to see a professional like a lawyer or an accountant. They don't understand the issues beyond what they see on television. It's the same when they meet with me for financial advice. It's a bewildering and alien process."

"In estate planning, they assume they need a very basic document—a will—and they often ask the lawyer, 'What does everybody typically do?' Then the herd mentality takes over. They all follow a boilerplate document and that is the end of the process," Rick said with a sigh.

"I think this Abundant Estate idea is smart. It will really help clients understand their choices and stay on course," smiled Jim. "Although, I did notice you spelled SMART wrong, college boy."

"The missing 'A' is for adaptability," laughed Rick. "It's implied, but thanks for the words of encouragement."

Rick continued, "I think we both agree that to get the most out of continuity planning, clients need to deepen and enhance their planning discussion with their advisors long *before* the will is even started. They must provide the lawyer with a clear sense of their goals and be able to articulate that vision. This allows the lawyer—from experience, skill and wisdom—to eliminate the 'false' choices, the solutions that are not appropriate for a particular client's strategic goals. It is only by following this kind of informed process that a professional can add real value while the client willingly signs an authentic document."

"This will be a challenge for all of us with Doug," added Jim.

"I tried to move him away from the tax discussion in relation to estate planning because that is a false choice," Rick stated. "Authentic intergenerational wealth-continuity planning is rarely done for tax reasons. The tax layer is almost last, or at least it should be. Rather than the starting point, tax planning should be a tactical technical solution used to further a clear strategy, which should, in turn, have been developed to achieve a bigger goal consistent with the client's mission and values."

"I get it," added Jim. "So taxes really should be an afterthought."

"It really depends, but often that is the case. It's important, but what's really most important is achieving the goals and objectives in furtherance of the family mission. You don't start with a tactic and create a goal; you execute on a goal with strategy and then tactics. That's the smart approach," said Rick.

He continued, "We also need to seize the moment in your relationship with Sarah, to move this whole planning discussion to a more strategic level."

"What do you mean?" said Jim, a little surprised.

"She was here today by a small miracle. Going forward, she always needs to be a part of your discussions with Doug. She is a stakeholder, and what we saw today is that he wants her to have that stake," stated Rick.

"I feel better now after the meeting. We are good . . . my rates of return with Doug have been excellent over the years," Jim stated with pride.

"Permission to speak candidly?" Rick asked.

"Granted," Jim chuckled.

"She won't give a rat's ass about returns if she thinks you weren't curious about her expectations and concerns. The statistics on retaining a spouse's account after the primary relationship dies are dismal. He's a lot older than her and he will almost certainly die first. If you don't start authentically engaging her now, then she's as good as gone when that time comes," said Rick.

"Well . . . ," stuttered Jim.

Rick continued, "Jim, people don't really care about statistics and numbers. They care about emotions and the bigger things in their lives. They care about how their choices make them feel. It's often said that people don't make decisions because of raw numbers, they need a story. Their goals are the narrative you want to reveal, understand, retell and bring to life."

"Good numbers are at least a signal of a successful tactical win though, right?" asked Jim.

"What's the goal?" asked Rick. "Do we even know that yet? I don't really know any of their values yet either. I can guess that a strong family will be one of them but, frankly, we haven't gotten that far. In jumping straight to goals without first discovering their values, there is a risk that we will do what *we* want for them rather than what they really want for themselves."

Jim realized they had only taken baby steps so far in the strategic engagement process. He didn't know the client's values, mission, goals or any other elements of the strategic process that would fill that void. "I feel like I have known Doug all my professional life and yet I really don't know a thing about him that is useful," he said with a tinge of despair in his voice. "That's terrible."

"Look," continued Rick, "Sarah signaled her personal engagement with this experience, and you saw that. That warm glow reflects on you more than you know. Now you have a beachhead established to start deepening this relationship. This type of strategic discussion is a great way to engage her with purpose. She needs to know that you are hearing her in these meetings we're having, and in all future meetings."

"I hope that he will let me," Jim said, referencing Doug.

"He already has," said Rick. "He revealed today that he has concerns for his whole family. He wants what's best for them. He trusts you and that level of trust is something you need to develop with Sarah. He may not say it, but he wants you to create it. That's why he is here and why she came along. This is a real breakthrough that you will look back on fifteen years from now and say, 'That's the moment I started working with this client instead of for this client.'"

"I think you're right," nodded Jim.

The two men parted and Rick returned to his office.

Rick circled around his desk and sat down with some force. He spun his chair around, put his feet up on the credenza and stared out the window that looked out over the city. The low sun provided some warmth and he shut his eyes and leaned back in his chair to think about the meeting that had just occurred. "All things considered, that went really well," he mused. "The Matthews are engaged in the process and Jim is amazing with the progress he is showing. A service-framing meeting was a suitable place to start. "Now the real journey begins," he said to himself, smiling.

• • •

Later in the afternoon, Rick's phone rang just as he was packing up to head home. It was Jim. He had just received a call from Doug's main legal advisor, Ross Packer. Ross wanted to meet Rick and Jim for lunch in the next few days if possible. Rick agreed to meet at 1 p.m. two days hence. Jim and Ross would coordinate the lunch location.

As he hung up with Jim, Rick noticed he had a text from Dave Milne:

Dave:
How is the lion's den, Danny-boy?

Rick texted back:

Rick:
Meeting a key client's lawyer. Going to discuss the new model and suggest that it's a better paradigm for planning.

Dave:
Go somewhere with plastic cutlery.

Rick:
LOL

Every client was surrounded by trusted advisors in a self-contained and mutually self-supporting advisory ecosystem. Rick understood that most people, including clients and their advisors, were uneasy with change. They preferred stasis to the uncertainty of introducing different participants and new ways of doing things. Rick's meeting with Ross Packer was every bit as important to the success of Doug's planning as was Jim's recent conversion to the Abundant Estate model. It was essential that every player in the ecosystem understood that the process was intended to divine the very best outcomes for the client. Rick needed to create a cohesive multidisciplinary team around Doug and Sarah that would work collaboratively towards fulfilling the strategic continuity goals of the Matthews family.

Rick's hard work was only just getting started. He decided that advisors needed some ground rules for strategic client engagement as well. He put down his bag and texted his wife that he would be late tonight. He needed to build a sensible model that advisors could use to think about how they delivered their value to their clients.

"If a client wants to use the Abundant Estate model," he thought to himself, "they will need an advisory team that has adopted a holistic and strategic approach to their service model. Otherwise, there will be a mismatch and the potential will wither on the vine."

Rick had recently attended a presentation at the Family Business x-Change on choosing the right family enterprise advisor. In that presentation, the suggestion was made that people should interview and select their professional advisory team based on aligned values as well as professional competence and other, more traditional, metrics. Rick flipped back to his notes and reviewed them. The skill set themes for any trusted advisor included:

- Self-awareness
- Trustworthy
- Servant leader
- Professional skill sets that were deep and broad

The speaker had also suggested that an advisor with deeply held values that were revealed in their work and lives was an indicator of alignment. A client authentically aligned on values with an advisor who also possessed the skills listed was truly well-served. A team of advisors aligned around a client was unstoppable. "The Abundant Estate loses power if any aspect of the process is not supported," Rick thought to himself. "Helping advisors see the benefits to the client and themselves is critical to success."

He reflected on his Abundant Estate model in relation to advisors and doodled a variety of ideas and constraints that were apparent and would need management. "I need to have steps or concepts that every advisor can employ. If it gets too specific to any one profession, it loses its universal message. It's up to the advisor to employ it as they may, but they need to understand the core elements that would be relevant for any professional," Rick thought to himself.

After an hour or so, he had cobbled together a good starting point:

The Abundant Estate for Advisors:

- Consider your client in the broadest sense to include: his or her spouse, children, grandchildren, business, advisor network and friends.
- Ask yourself whether you can adapt your process so that every client relationship gets the benefit of a fiercely curious and holistic mindset.
- Adopt an abundance mentality. Every client relationship deserves candor and selflessness. Be prepared to lose the client if he or she rejects your process. They will find another advisor and you will attract more appropriate work from other clients.
- With genuine curiosity, seek to understand the full breadth and depth of each client's situation and their goals.
- Engage a strategic approach to planning and create an authentic timeline to review your understanding of the client's situation—values, mission, goals, objectives, strategies and tactics—on a regular basis.
- Conduct yourself as if you will be invited to give the eulogy for every client when he or she dies.

Rick reflected on his thoughts and decided it was a good start. This model for advisors also had the ability to function as an assessment tool for clients. For example, a client could ask their advisor to describe how they engage stakeholders in their planning process. They could ask for clarity on the specific strategic model the advisor uses with clients and how they would seek to manage a conflict if there was a disagreement with the process.

"That's what the advisor at Holistic didn't do when Sarah asked about specific process," thought Rick. "If advisors are thinking in this manner, then they will be receptive to more fulsome planning with the clients, such as following my Abundant Estate model. Moreover, if an advisor is committed to this type of a model, then clients will truly feel that the advisor is a full partner in their strategic journey. They will be a part of the story."

He saved the list before closing down the computer and headed to the elevator. As he waited for it to arrive, he thought to himself, "This will be tricky for some advisors. For clients, too, because it demands that they be proactive in selecting advisors beyond the usual metrics of investment performance or a pleasing personality. They have to understand their goals and process expectations and choose an advisor that aligns with those demands. It's really different. In some cases, they may need to form new relationships to stay within the model."

Rick emerged from the basement parking into the brilliant last rays of sunshine for the day. The complete model had finally come together and he was excited about the prospects for change that lay ahead.

Chapter 6
Aligning the Advisory Team

"I am firm. You are obstinate. He is a pig-headed fool."
—Bertrand Russell

THE DAY HAD ARRIVED for lunch with Doug's lawyer, Ross Packer. At 12:30 p.m., Rick's phone alarm reminded him of the meeting and Rick packed up his desk to set out for the restaurant. He had printed off some copies of his evolving Abundant Estate model, including the newest element for advisors, in the event Ross wanted to explore it further in the conversation.

Ross and Jim were already at the Blue Moon restaurant when Rick arrived. Jim had ordered some appetizers for the table and was enjoying a jovial laugh with Ross when he got up to welcome Rick.

"Rick, I want to introduce you to my friend Ross Packer," said Jim as Rick and Ross shook hands.

"It's very nice to meet you, Rick," said Ross. "Doug told me some good things about his meeting with you the other day."

"I'm glad you had the chance to connect. He's a really nice man. I especially appreciated meeting his wife, Sarah. She adds a lot to the conversation," said Rick.

"I hope nobody minds, but I invited Doug's accountant to join us today as well. He will be here after lunch for a coffee. His name is Alf Schurton. Good guy for a bean counter," laughed Ross.

They all enjoyed a good chuckle and set about reviewing the restaurant's menu.

"Rick and I have just started working with Doug on his estate—I mean, wealth-continuity planning. It has been a really interesting process for me; we are moving to a more holistic approach to the planning, strategy, goals, creating a sense of family values. It's exciting," said Jim.

"He won't go for that, Jim. He's old school. The plan is to just keep it simple and get the assets out to the kids; it's their problem if they mess it up. You're wasting your time. Is it Sarah or Kelly pushing for this?" asked Ross rather dismissively.

Rick and Jim were taken aback at Ross's cavalier attitude.

Rick decided to explore the apparent pushback. "Well, actually, Doug is interested in this type of approach," he added. "I don't know what he was like twenty years ago, but he seems to be in a different mental space today. He and Sarah are concerned about the effect the wealth will have on their family in terms of motivation and family dynamics. They seem very likely to want information about preparing heirs to be good stewards of financial wealth. I think they're ready for an updated approach in their planning program."

"I have to say, Ross, that's what I'm hearing too. He called me after the meeting and said he was also worried about there being enough financial wealth to carry forward into future generations," added Jim.

"Rick, let me tell you something, I have been doing this a long, long time. What makes you think you can plan to avoid those outcomes? A trust? An annuity? A corporation? Sure, they structure the gifts, but the beneficiaries will be beneficiaries. They are who they are, and we are just complicating things by adding all this purposeful stuff. It will just end up in court and everybody will get sued. Plus, you know how tax-oriented he is, he won't give a hoot about the sustainability aspect, he's always been about keeping it simple and cost-efficient," said Ross, inserting a large, butter-soaked bun into his mouth.

Just then, the accountant, Alf, came to the table and introduced himself to Rick and Jim. His meeting had ended early and he came straight to the restaurant. Rick didn't know Alf and Jim had connected with him only via e-mail and phone to discuss Doug's year-end tax planning. He was younger than everyone at the table and had just replaced a retiring partner who had been Doug's long-standing advisor. Alf signaled to the waitstaff for a menu and quickly ordered the fish tacos while the others confirmed their selections.

"We were just discussing how the tax planning for Doug will really drive the estate-planning piece; that's always been the focus for Doug," said Ross to Alf.

Rick glanced at Jim with a smile. "That was a self-serving mischaracterization," he thought.

"Well, that's a typical starting point and he does lean that way. Where are you in the process?" asked Alf of Rick.

"Truthfully, we are very early in the process. Jim and I have been developing a strategic model to use with Doug and all future clients that is more holistic about client advice and engagement. I call it the Abundant Estate," said Rick as he passed a copy of the document he had brought to Alf and Ross.

"This would be interesting to me," added Alf, glancing at the handout from Rick. "Good for you, Jim. Your clients will really benefit from that model. I have come to believe that a purposeful, goals-based approach is the best way to deal with client planning. I also think it's great we are all here today. I have recently done some family business advisor training and I am convinced that this type of multidisciplinary approach is the key to effective planning."

"I am not sure what that means, Alf," said a slightly exasperated Ross, spraying bits of crusty bun everywhere as he spoke. "We always share information on clients, you write up the needed steps and I execute and advise on the legal aspects of the various steps in the process. What more do we need to do? I mean, really, we get the work done very fast and cost-effectively."

Rick just kept watching and listening to the conversation, waiting for the right moment to add some perspective. Jim seemed unusually quiet as he listened to the accountant and lawyer banter.

"It's not good enough anymore, Ross. We can and need to do more. First of all, working on strategy as a team ensures that the client gets the best outcome because all the goals and tactical bases are integrated and aligned. But we need to be there at the start, too," said Alf, gesturing to everyone at the table. "There will likely be other professionals we should include as well, given the complexity of Doug's enterprise wealth."

"The start? What do you mean?" asked Ross. He was clearly bewildered by the conversation. He buttered a second Portuguese bun as he spoke.

"Maybe I can share some of what we have been discussing," said Rick, pointing to himself and Jim. As he said that, he reached into his briefcase and took out the list of suggestions for advisors he had created a few nights earlier:

The Abundant Estate for Advisors:

- Consider your client in the broadest sense to include: his or her spouse, children, grandchildren, business, advisor network and friends.
- Ask yourself whether you can adapt your process so that every client relationship gets the benefit of a fiercely curious and holistic mindset.
- Adopt an abundance mentality. Every client relationship deserves candor and selflessness. Be prepared to lose the client if he or she rejects your process. They will find another advisor and you will attract more appropriate work from other clients.
- With genuine curiosity, seek to understand the full breadth and depth of each client's situation and their goals.
- Engage a strategic approach to planning and create an authentic timeline to review your understanding of the client's situation—values, mission, goals, objectives, strategies and tactics—on a regular basis.
- Conduct yourself as if you will be invited to give the eulogy for every client when he or she dies.

"Sorry, Jim, I worked this out late the other night and we really haven't had any chance to walk through it yet. But I think you will see that the pieces fit neatly into our engagement with Doug," said Rick as he shared the information.

Jim, Alf and Ross looked at it together for a moment.

"Well, that's hard for me to do," Ross said in a dismissive tone. "I advise the individual or the company. Professionally, it's a challenge to advise a whole group. You know, Rick, there are many potential conflicts of interest when giving legal advice to all the members of a family. That's risky for me and for them. I am also pretty skeptical that it needs to be this complicated. It's just estate planning. I mean, you do a will and move the assets to the children. In this case, they are all competent adults. It should be pretty simple. Doug won't want trusts. My experience with other clients is that simple works best," finished Ross.

"Works best for whom?" smiled Alf.

Ross seemed mildly agitated by the implication of the question, so Rick interrupted. "This approach helps to ensure that the assets stay intact and the stated goals of the family are achieved. That's where I can add value to your work, Ross; I can meet the whole family and understand their collective and individual goals. This helps us to create a unique strategic plan for the wealth. The issue really is that a good process can be constructed using other professionals who don't have the constraints you have, which are entirely legitimate."

"That takes me out of the loop," sputtered Ross.

"Not at all," said Alf. "It keeps you in the loop and always at the table. It just changes the starting points for the conversation. I would suggest it puts you in a better place because you can weave your magic in response to fulfilling the deeply considered and openly communicated goals of the client."

"Well," Ross conceded after some thought, "I have to admit that secrets and poor communication usually lead to misunderstandings and conflict. I don't like that for my clients, and sometimes the solutions we provide are created in an information vacuum. That upsets beneficiaries. You know, their mother passes away and they find out there is this restrictive trust over the assets, and they freak out and look for people to blame. It gets messy."

"We can't promise that won't happen, but we should at least try to add elements to the planning process that will offer some glimmer of hope that we tried our best to avoid those consequences," added Rick.

Ross seemed to reluctantly nod his agreement.

"We will be looking to understand the goals and objectives of the family members so that we, as technical experts, can build the strategies and tactics appropriate to achieve those goals. It's a powerful process," added Jim enthusiastically.

"But we all need to be part of that goal-building process," said Alf.

"Agreed," said Rick.

"Look, boys, I'm going to call bullshit on this idea," said Ross. "The purpose of estate planning is to move the assets of the estate to the heirs quickly and cost efficiently. There are no beneficiaries who require special attention in Doug's situation. And it really doesn't matter what the children want, it's Doug's money to give. They have no input at all in this process. It just clouds the water to bring them in. What am I . . . a social worker? We are taking something simple and making it more complicated than it needs to be."

"With respect, Ross, I think that attitude is the problem. We all tend to look at estate planning as an event, but it is a process. I spent years advising my business-owner clients and was usually looking in the rear-view mirror. We did some planning for the future, but it was typically isolated to the tax silo. Then, one client situation made me doubt that approach as sufficient," said Alf.

"What happened?" asked Rick.

"We did some corporate share planning and gave common shares to the children in order to achieve a tax outcome," explained Alf. "It reduced the income tax but was very confusing to the family. They weren't sure if they were trusted owners or mere tax pawns. It came to a head when one of the sons started a divorce proceeding.

The sisters not involved in the business became worried about the viability of the business and decided that they were owners of the company and wanted their share—right then and there. They were very jealous of the relationship the son had with their mother, as both mother and son were involved in the business. The trouble was that the family had never discussed the *purpose* of the planning. The mother, who owned the company, just did the share reorganization without any consultation. She felt she could do as she pleased because she lived by the golden rule."

"She who has the gold, makes the rules," laughed Rick.

"That's it," said Alf. "The sisters felt they were simply tax tools to enhance the financial well-being of their brother. It was terrible, and the subsequent litigation did damage to the family relations and that was a surprise to me; I didn't see it coming. Frankly, I never gave it any consideration at all," he finished.

"Well, family businesses are a minefield anyway. You can't stop that from happening," added Ross. "If they are going to fight, they are going to fight."

"I am not sure I agree with that, Ross," said Rick. "I appreciate that family enterprises are complex and dynamic environments, but I think that simply reinforces Alf's point—we need to approach that type of situation as a team. No one professional will see or solve all their issues. We need to show them how to manage conflict before it ends up in court."

Jim seemed unsettled that Rick was disagreeing with his old friend.

Alf, however, was just getting started. "I have to agree with Rick," he said. "The problem I had with that client was that I was very prescriptive in my work. I saw a tactical solution, and that's where we went. The family just glommed on to the tidy structure because it avoided exposing the real issues and the heavy lifting that would be needed to address their family's core problems. If I had spent more time working on understanding their true goals and understanding the dynamics of their family enterprise, I may have done something different. No, I *know* I would have done it differently."

Ross was changing colors now. He started to fulminate a bit. "Look, the client comes to us and describes a situation that needs to be fixed, they come to us for our advice. We give it to the best of our professional ability. What 'different' can you possibly do, Alf?" he sputtered.

"Well, for starters, I challenge clients a little more when they describe their situations. I used to accept their assessment of a situation as the truth. However, I am seeing now that people tend to be overly optimistic and understate the risk in their family and business systems. For example, when it comes to judging whether their children will be interested in certain assets or taking over a business. Also, in judging the status of a child's marriage or financial acumen. They see their children through a very special lens," Alf stated.

"Gentlemen, if I don't accept the word of my client, what am I to do? Hire a private investigator, like Magnum P.I.?" asked Ross. "That said, Hawaii is looking pretty good right now."

They all chuckled, and Ross himself smiled as the mood lightened.

Their lunches arrived and they spent a few minutes enjoying the food and sharing some war stories. Rick observed that Ross's disposition had changed and he seemed more at ease with his tablemates as they shared their experiences. There was some small talk about recent tax changes. They also discussed a few high-level matters related to Doug's situation where there was a common interest. As they finished eating, Rick observed a more contemplative mood descend upon Ross as Jim was updating the table on Kelly and Todd.

"So, tell me about the fish," Ross said to Alf.

Alf seemed surprised by the question and choked a bit. He reached for his water and started laughing.

"Why are you choking? They do excellent perch here. The fish tacos were an excellent choice," chuckled Ross.

"I thought you meant FISH accounts in holistic planning," coughed Alf.

"What?" asked Ross.

"He means to say that a family's wealth is not just financial when we take a long-term view of their continuity planning," interjected Rick. "It means all of the financial, intellectual, social and human capital that exists in the family."

"It was a topic at last month's estate-planning council meeting," gasped Alf.

"I do recognize that topic now. Any relevance to Doug's situation?" Ross asked.

"Well," started Rick, "he has some concerns about the sustainability of his financial wealth long term and the future ability of his heirs to steward and grow that wealth. He wants the money to provide growth in the family, I would suggest. Not in absolute numbers of course, but in terms of opportunity, potential and stability."

Finally recovered, Alf added, "There is a belief that successful intergenerational wealth transfer is best achieved when families accept that the primary purpose of financial wealth is to invest in and nurture each family member's intellectual, social and human capacities. That is likely a conversation and exploration that Doug and Sarah will eventually have with us in this approach."

The group continued to discuss the FISH accounts and how that was a radical departure from the usual consideration that family wealth meant only financial assets. Rick observed that Ross asked many thoughtful questions and seemed genuinely interested in the concept.

After clearing the lunch dishes, the waitstaff brought coffees and espressos to the table.

"Alf, tell me a little more about how you perceive multidisciplinary advising to work. The reason I ask is that I noticed some coaches and family business advisors speaking on that topic at our local estate-planning association over the last year or so. I didn't go because it looked too fluffy, but maybe I should have attended after all," said Ross.

Alf described how he used a new process to engage the entire family when he was working on wealth or business transition. Gone were the days when he would only ever deal with the founder or owner. He interviewed all members of the family in an effort to understand the dynamics of the business, management and family. If possible, he liked to do that with the lawyer and other key advisors present at strategic points.

"Well, who's in charge, man? I mean, how does stuff get done?" asked Ross.

Rick jumped in, "It gets done by the relevant professional when it is the appropriate time in the process for the work to be completed. As to who's in charge, the family and the advisors can collectively decide on that aspect. A process champion is really helpful and it could come from the family and the advisory team. It may well be different depending on the advisors and their respective interest in being a process leader. That's the key: no single advisor is more important than any other. They function as a team. And if there is a leader, they are in that role because they are prepared to be servants to the family and the process."

Ross seemed unsure. "So you interview all the family members as well? How are their opinions relevant?" he asked of Alf.

"I do," said Alf. "With the permission and understanding of the owners, of course. It depends on who reaches out for guidance. I work very hard to frame their expectations and ensure their agreement on which parties will be invited to participate. The more we engage, the better the outcome."

Rick interjected, "I strive to do the same thing with parents who are preparing their estate plans. With their permission, I'll interview everybody who has a stake in the successful outcome of the process so that I understand their individual and collective priorities and values."

"Why are you interested in what the children want?" asked Ross. "I mean, they should just be thankful to receive a gift from their parents, right?"

"I think there is much more to it than that nowadays, Ross," said Rick. "Preparing heirs to be good wealth stewards and to be able to lead full and happy lives demands a purposeful and strategic approach to the wealth-planning process. We can't just assume that more money means more happiness. To put it in Doug's terms, he wants to be sure that the next generations are not negatively affected by the access to financial wealth. How would you solve that stated estate-planning goal?"

Ross thought for a moment before responding. "I'm not sure. A restrictive trust, I suppose."

Rick observed that Ross offered this tactical solution with little excitement. He seemed to appreciate that it may not come close to achieving the core goal. "I would approach it this way," he told Ross. "I would be interested in the values and goals of the whole family to try and build a sense of shared responsibility for, and ownership of, the plan. In those cases, if we do it right, we empower the entire family to be in charge. They begin to drive the collective priorities and create their own processes. They also plan with greater purpose and realize that financial wealth is there to be invested in the human, social and intellectual capital of the family. This is a way of preserving wealth for generations and avoiding the 'shirtsleeves to shirtsleeves' and 'affluenza' dilemmas."

That last comment caught Ross's attention, and he stared thoughtfully at Rick for a moment.

Alf chimed in again, "Obviously, some items will be front burner and that's where a professional's assessment is so vital. But we can add even more value in other, less urgent parts of the process, and that's another key thing I would have done differently with that tax case. I would have spent time developing strong family communication and authentic governance. When the poop hit the fan on the divorce, they had no way of coping to manage the conflict. They didn't have sufficient communication skills, and family concerns crossed into business concerns and the situation quickly spun out of control. Knowing what I know now, I would have done a better job there."

"Well, you aren't a family therapist, Alf," said Jim.

"No, I'm not. I'm also not a lawyer, financial advisor, trust officer, insurance specialist, mediator or facilitator. Sometimes a man has got to know his limitations," he laughed.

"So, you are engaged from the get-go?" Ross asked Alf.

"Well, it depends. Sometimes the families work extensively with someone like Rick to create a values matrix so they can start to advance into a strategic planning process like his Abundant Estate model. I might use a facilitator or coach in those situations if I'm the one who gets the ball rolling. I will still be part of it, though. I think it's good practice. Then I move from being a mere order-taker to being a true trusted advisor. It's a much better position to be in because I can add real value, not just technical expertise," added Alf.

"The research is pretty clear, Ross. The likelihood of long-term success for a technical solution is greatly increased if it is accompanied with and integrated into a legitimate process that fosters, among other things, both effective communication and independent governance," said Rick.

Ross seemed to scoff a little as he sipped his coffee. Jim smiled and added, "Rick, what does that really mean, 'communication and governance'?"

Alf jumped in and said, "It's simple, really. Governance is just another way of saying decision-making and, in that sense, each family needs to develop their own unique process for it. How does this family make decisions? Do they have the trust of one another, in themselves and in a process, to deal with issues as they arise and to communicate to make effective decisions?"

"All right, the jargon's out of the way, let's frame this within Doug's situation. He was pretty pissed when he called me the other day. He didn't seem at all sure what was going on and what the outcome was supposed to be. I think I'm starting to see where you're taking him now," said Ross.

"He was pissed off?" asked a nervous Jim.

"Well," stopped Ross. "Those are my words, I suppose. He was certainly a little agitated."

Alf stepped in, "He's likely just a little uncertain. Fear often reveals itself as anger. He's used to calling the shots on everything. He assesses the lay of the land and makes the decisions himself. Maybe that approach doesn't work so well anymore and he is unsure a bit?

People lash out when they feel out of control. Maybe the dynamics of his relationship with Sarah have changed all the communications and decision-making in the home."

With his eyes lowered, Ross was listening intently and slowly stirring a third sugar into an espresso. "You know," he began, "maybe you're right and we haven't evolved enough to meet him where he is. He has a very strained relationship with his daughter, Kelly. Gabrielle's death destroyed him, and Kelly headed to Hawaii for good after the funeral. Jim, you and Doug are about the same age as me. Do you ever reflect back and think about your choices in life? I know I do. I wonder if he is doing the same thing?"

Alf let the conversation pause for a moment before jumping in, "That is a really critical insight, Ross. As advisors, we need to meet our clients where they actually are. How can we know that if we don't spend time uncovering the goals and aspirations of the entire family? I mean, the reality is, the client is a sibling, a parent, a spouse, an employer, a community leader—he or she wears many outfits. The important thing is that we try to get a full understanding of what's underneath the costumes to really understand the situation, the family dynamics and the client's goals. We need to be courageous enough to take the client into the difficult waters. That way, we build plans *with* them, instead of just *for* them. Going through the process together builds their planning skills and allows them to deal with change and conflict in more productive ways on their own and within the family."

"People resist change, Ross," said Rick. "My experience has been, and I am certain yours is similar, that people avoid planning because it acknowledges looming change. They procrastinate, focus on the simple matters or low-hanging fruit that can be quickly fixed, and never deal with the core issues. For example, in Doug's case, his relationship with Kelly. I haven't learned enough yet but, as a father, I can hardly imagine that level of estrangement from a child. The idea of addressing it creates a fear of the unknown. He doesn't know if it will be better or worse, so he keeps it all the same."

Ross softly nodded his agreement.

Rick continued, "I also believe that people avoid planning because they can imagine only the bad things that will happen. They will have tremendous regret for the situation that their planning caused and, because it was their own plan, they may have to wear responsibility for the outcomes, which are far from certain."

"So, you are suggesting they might prefer to allow a disaster to occur by not doing anything, rather than be responsible for whatever occurs when they actually do something proactive?" asked Alf.

"I think it's just human nature," Rick responded. "If we don't do anything and bad stuff happens, it's a lot easier to lay the blame on the victims of the lack of planning, in this case, the beneficiaries. They must be responsible for their own misfortune because they were greedy or bad people. I think that's what we are really saying when we assume a family business will blow up as it transitions from one generation to another. Blame the latter generations, it was their fault."

"That's a good insight, Rick," added Alf. "When, in fact, the main culprit was the failure to plan purposefully in the first place in each generation. We have to help clients adopt processes that spread out the responsibility for the consequences of decisions made, so everyone will feel engaged and that they share the responsibility. This is how we get people to take action."

Rick added, "That's likely why half of North American adults don't have a will. It's a plan, and they become responsible for that plan the moment the documents are signed. If they don't plan, they don't bear the responsibility. I think the Abundant Estate helps them get through that wall of inaction."

"I see a lot of unsigned shareholder agreements as well," added Ross under his breath. "I am sure a similar gremlin is at work in those situations."

They all began to put on their jackets and get up to leave the restaurant. Alf and Rick exchanged business cards while Ross and Jim spoke quietly near the door. Rick was really excited about the direction this day had taken. The advisors weren't all converts yet, but they were starting to see where change and collaboration were both possible and desirable.

As Rick and Jim returned to their office, Jim began speaking, "I was talking to Ross there. He wasn't completely sure of the terrain we are on, but he thinks it's worth a try with Doug."

"Why the change of heart?" asked Rick.

"Doug is our friend and our client. I care what happens to him, and Ross could see that was our focus. There is no product to sell here, this is about doing the right thing. When he said we should meet Doug where he is, he was thinking about Kelly. That was a sour outcome for Doug. Ross has a daughter as well, about the same age as Kelly. She is the light of his life and they have a great relationship. It pains him to see Doug losing that gift," said a thoughtful Jim.

"Well, we can help Doug see that there are resources available to help him mend that damage," said Rick. "Maybe it can't be fully repaired at all and he has to want it fixed, so does Kelly. In reality, we can't make people change until they are ready to change and want to take those steps. But, that all said, I really believe that we do a better job of wealth management and wealth-continuity planning if we acknowledge these matters. Simply bolting a technical solution, like a will or trust, onto a dynamic situation will be no help and may even do more harm than good."

"I think that was Alf's point with the company he described," added Jim. "They applied a static tax solution onto a volatile family situation they hadn't even started to try and understand."

"That just doesn't work, and if it does, it's pure luck," sighed Rick. "What we are really trying to achieve is a form of dynamic stability. The underlying problems cannot be ignored even though they may never be truly solved. This is where good process is your friend. Good process will help you manage the dynamics so that the entire family ecosystem can maintain greater stability."

"Ross was concerned he would end up out of the loop. Our lunch today convinced him that he is very much a key member in the loop," added Jim.

"Advisors are people, too. They don't much like change either. It has to be managed sometimes because change happens no matter what, it is life's only constant. A gift our interaction can provide is a method for managing change. The family can respond to change purposefully, as an opportunity for growth and regeneration," said Rick.

"I was worried there for a minute when I heard Doug was pissed," said Jim. They had arrived at Jim's office and they sat down for a moment to chat. "Ross exaggerated a little for sure. But, then I thought about it a little more and I realized that Doug wasn't angry at us, he was struggling to deal with the changes in play. Sarah is exerting herself in the planning in a manner that Gabrielle never did. Also, it's a blended family, which can be complicated to consider. Estate planning probably felt easier when Gabrielle was alive because their interests were so obviously aligned and focused on the children. It's different the second time around."

"Even that has evolved," added Rick.

"I can hardly imagine how that feels," said Jim.

"What happened with Kelly, anyway?" asked Rick.

"Truthfully, I am not totally sure. She is fiercely strong-willed, like her father. They always seemed to be at odds over something or other. I have always assumed that she was so much like him, that they naturally butted heads," said Jim.

"But she didn't like his business?" asked Rick.

"Well, she is a passionate environmentalist and his company was cited a few times as a polluter when she was in high school. Strangely enough, they aren't even in that industry anymore, but the damage was done, I guess," said Jim.

"So, nothing to do with Sarah at all?" asked Rick.

"I am not sure. Maybe," added Jim with some uncertainty. "It's probably a rich tapestry of emotions."

"What about Todd? Does Kelly get on with Todd?" asked Rick.

"I think there is friction there. He went right into the business from high school and she went to university. Todd and Doug are tight. They are very different personalities, but they get on well. Todd does what he is told," said Jim.

"And Kelly never did," added Rick.

"Not so much," Jim replied.

"Well, we can't change the past, but purposeful planning demands that we help the family create new ways to manage the future. That is useful information. I think we can build on that for Doug's planning. He has a lot of moving parts in his life, no wonder he is ill at ease with the conversation. He has no idea what will happen at his death . . . and I think he cares a lot," said Rick.

"We need to get more information," said Jim.

Rick concurred, and they agreed to have Sarah and Doug in for another meeting as soon as possible to start the Abundant Estate process.

Rick went back to his office and stared out the window across the city. A thunderstorm had passed over while they were at lunch, and it was moving now to the east. The sun's rays began to split resplendently through the remaining clouds at the back end of the storm.

He reflected on the lunch meeting and the journey ahead for Doug, Sarah and all of their advisors. There were going to be bumps and scratches along the way. The dynamics of long-standing relationships would be altered as new processes and participants entered the Matthews' family. Rick knew it would be an ongoing challenge to get the clients to take ownership of their planning in a strategic and purposeful manner. It was going to be hard work and very often a slow process. Yet, he knew this was the right path for these clients and he was excited to take the next step with them in the engagement process.

Chapter 7
Purposeful Wealth

"I went to a bookstore and asked the saleswoman, 'Where's the self-help section?' She said if she told me, it would defeat the purpose."

—*George Carlin*

A WEEK PASSED after Rick's lunch meeting with Doug's advisors. He plowed ahead on other files that he had started before he created the Abundant Estate model. He tried at every opportunity to bring his new approach into the discussion wherever possible. It was tricky, but several of the families were very receptive to starting again with purpose in mind. From time to time, he circled back to the Matthews matter as new ideas and thoughts popped into his head.

On Wednesday, Rick received a phone call from Ross Packer's assistant at the law firm Keon & Clark. She was wondering if Rick was available to meet Ross the following day for lunch at Wendel's Roastery, next door to their law office. As it turned out, Rick had just had a cancellation for an out-of-town meeting scheduled for that day, so he happily accepted.

After hanging up, Rick pondered the purpose of the meeting request. It was almost certainly about the Matthews's planning, but he suspected that something more was afoot. Sensing danger, he texted Dave for some advice.

Rick:

You there?

Several minutes later, Dave texted back:

Dave:

What's up?

Rick:

Client's lawyer wants meeting after team conversation last week. My spidey senses are tingling. Any advice?

The phone rang several seconds later. It was Dave.

"That was fast," said Rick.

"Well, it's getting juicy now," replied Dave. "I wanted to hear the scoop directly from you. What's he want?"

"I'm not sure," said Rick. "Although it's definitely about the client. They are old friends. There was a point in our discussion when I mentioned FISH accounts and avoiding the 'shirtsleeves to shirtsleeves' dilemma. He seemed to take special note of both concepts, but we moved on in the conversation. I wonder if it's that?"

"Was he receptive?" Dave asked.

"He wasn't at first, but that seemed to change by the end. Jim said he was softened by the emphasis on using the process to mend or better manage the relationship between the client and his daughter."

"Strained, is it?" Dave inquired.

"It sounded like it was," Rick responded. "Although I sensed it was not beyond recovery. Ross, the lawyer, is in a reflective mood. There may be some breakthroughs possible here."

"The FISH concept is unusual," said Dave. "It will toss him for a loop. But it's a key building block to effective planning. Will you review that with him?"

Rick thought about this for a moment and then said, "I think I will prepare a short explanation so that he sees the way it fits into my strategic model."

"Maybe he was intrigued by avoiding 'shirtsleeves to shirtsleeves?'" suggested Dave.

"That may well be it. He is a corporate lawyer and works with a lot of business-owner families. I bet he sees a lot of challenging situations."

"Make sure he is your ally. Is he your ally?"

Rick chuckled. "I'm not sure why I need to worry about him as an ally. Why do you say that?"

"Did you see the *The Godfather?*" asked Dave. "Do you remember Abe Vigoda's character, Tessio?"

"Of course," said Rick. "Vigoda played the character of Fish on TV, too, but that's not what we're talking about here. . . ."

"I didn't even think of that. Ha!" laughed Dave. "No, Tessio is a capo in the Corleone family. He betrays Michael Corleone, and the treason is revealed when he is the first to suggest a peace conference on his turf after the transition caused by the Godfather's death."

"Hmm . . . that's the smart move," mused Rick. "Isolate to sabotage the process. I hadn't thought of that. I didn't get that impression though."

"Be careful that Ross stays engaged and connected. He may be the gatekeeper," advised Dave. "Hey, is Abe Vigoda finally dead?"

Rick smiled at the reference and said, "Sadly, yes. He finally is."

The two friends said goodbye and Rick set to work creating a quick handout on FISH to share with Ross in their meeting, just in case.

"Okay," Rick thought to himself as he typed, "FISH is an acronym for the various types of family capital or wealth, including **F**inancial, **I**ntellectual, **S**ocial and **H**uman. Those are the four main sources of wealth or capital a person has to plan with in his or her life." He drafted a table with basic definitions:

Type of Wealth or Capital	Definition[1]
Financial	Liquid investments, insurance, business enterprise assets, art work, websites and social media, real estate, licenses, intellectual property such as patents, copyrights and trademarks. All of these items can be sold for cash or can be retained and leveraged to create cash flow.

Intellectual	What the family knows, including content and processes associated with sustaining the other forms of wealth, family stories and collective wisdom from experiences. In a knowledge-based economy, this may be the most important source of capital.
Social	One definition of social capital characterizes it as the relationships between individuals and organizations that facilitate action and create value.[2]
Human	This form of capital can assume many investable forms, including innate and learned skills and abilities, personality, reputation and credentials.

"That's a good starting point for our meeting. I can discuss with Ross how it's vital to invest the financial assets of the client into the intellectual, social and human capital of the family. The only reason financial capital assets exist at all is to serve the creators positively, and those whom they wish to benefit," thought Rick as he printed off the table for the meeting. "If we focus too much or exclusively on the financial assets, we risk wasting all of the sources of family wealth, including the financial." He also reviewed a few articles and sections of books he had ear-marked over time, refreshing his memory on key points to raise with Ross. He was assuming that the idea of strategic continuity planning and the Abundant Estate approach would be the topics of discussion, and he wanted to be prepared.

• • •

The next day, Rick walked into Wendel's, where he was to meet Ross at 11 a.m. As was his custom, he arrived fifteen minutes early, grabbed a coffee and claimed the best booth in the place, at the back overlooking the park. He reviewed his various notes regarding Doug, including the FISH table in case it was needed. He wanted Ross to be an ally rather than an obstacle.

At exactly 11:00, Ross ambled in with a briefcase and wheeled litigation bag in tow. He looked pretty haggard. Rick got up to shake his hand and they both sat down. Rick offered to grab a couple of coffees at the front while Ross settled in. When he returned, Ross had pulled out a piece of paper of his own with various notes and a list of what appeared to be questions.

"Just getting back from court?" asked Rick, nodding to the litigation bag on wheels.

"Yes," answered Ross. "The part of my work I don't really enjoy, but it's a necessary evil."

"You don't like to do court work?" asked Rick. He himself had done a few years of litigation and was happy to exit that field. Moreover, the litigation community was equally thrilled he had departed.

"I do it to pay the bills. Frankly, it has always rubbed my fur the wrong way. I am not certain that it is a process that advances the best interests of my business clients. Nobody wants to litigate, but there is often no alternative," said Ross as he sipped on his coffee and gathered his composure.

"I did it just long enough to know I didn't want to do it," laughed Rick. "The universe of litigation clients is far better off with me outside their ecosystem."

"I saw your profile on LinkedIn, it looks like you had that epiphany early in your career. That's lucky. Knowing what you like early is a giant bonus in a career path. We should all be able to do what we love and love what we do," added Ross.

Rick was surprised Ross was even on LinkedIn. He was further shocked that Ross had creeped his profile. "What took you to my LinkedIn profile?" Rick inquired.

"Frankly, I was trying to figure out where you were coming from in your discussions with Doug and Sarah. I went to some of the websites of the associations and organizations on your profile and found them quite interesting. I find that understanding is improved when the contextual views of the parties are better understood," added Ross. "That's why I wanted to chat today. I am intrigued by what you are doing with Doug. I want to understand it better."

"What part intrigues you?" asked a now very curious and surprised Rick.

"Well, for starters, you must understand that Doug and I are friends as well as lawyer and client. I have a lot of reasons to want to see him do well and be happy. I have been doing his business work for more years than I care to recall. He trusts me a great deal, and that is really important to me as his lawyer and as his friend," started Ross.

"Yet?" prompted Rick.

Ross paused for a moment. He looked down at his papers and curled the edges a bit. He seemed a little uncertain. "Yet," he started, "I may be out of my expert area for where he needs to go. His concerns are not what I am used to dealing with. I am starting to work with him on his business-succession planning, to hand the company over to Todd, and he is very reluctant to move ahead. The planning is technically solid and he will save a whack of tax, but we can't get him to execute the documents or even convene a meeting to set a firm timetable. He's always too busy or there is some drama that takes precedence that day."

"How long has this been going on?" asked Rick.

"Four years," laughed Ross. "Four years and the best I can say is we are getting started."

"There is research to support the idea that even the most technically sound succession plan, be it for personal wealth or business, is at substantial risk of failure if it isn't supported by authentic and sustainable communication, independent governance and a strategic process. He's a smart guy, is it possible he senses that what is being proposed is not really addressing the main problem or concern he has with the situation?" asked Rick.

"So, maybe we are answering the questions *we* need answered rather than the ones *he* wants answered," mused Ross.

"And he doesn't even know how to ask them or how to frame his actual concerns," said Rick. Something is blocking his decision-making. Maybe pride, fear of regret, diminished status, lack of purpose, embarrassment—so many reasons are possible. I have always thought an unsigned will or shareholder agreement reflects a document that is not trusted by the parties. It isn't real to them, not authentically theirs, and they don't trust what it would create or do for their relationships. Family businesses are so dynamic, have you explored the three-circle model of family-business systems?"

Ross said he had heard of it but had not spent any time exploring it in great detail.

Rick turned the tray liner over and began to draw the three circles in a family enterprise: management, ownership and family. He explained how each circle represented an independent system of individuals, norms, expectations and relationships. When the circles were drawn in the manner of a Venn diagram, overlapping and intersecting with one another, he illustrated that some people were players in a couple circles, or even in all three.

"They have to wear two or more hats in the same family business," said Rick. "That causes confusion in matters of perspective."

"So when Mom is also the general manager," started Ross, "which hat is she wearing when she praises or criticizes a family member at work? I see: this is a tool to help build clarity around forms of communication and decision-making for a family business. To deal with those areas of overlap on the drawing."

Rick explained how, as a consultant, his role was to generate clarity on processes and content in the areas where the circles overlapped and where there were paradoxical relationships or expectations.

"That was the intellectual basis of the training Alf mentioned as well," added Rick.

He continued, "I use the exploratory procedures around the three-circle tool to create family and business mission statements. They can lead to the strategic model I shared with you or a similar type of approach with the business side of the equation. Sometimes, in the process of articulating values and creating a mission statement, we are able to establish more authentic shareholder considerations that really reflect the family. No legalese, no techie tax mumbo-jumbo. We just have a plain-language series of statements that give flesh to the shareholder agreement. More people sign after that type of process because they all understand the real parameters of consensus."

"Doug may appreciate and benefit from that approach," suggested Ross. "Something is causing him to be stuck."

"One good approach is to use this model of inquiry to systematically chip away at the things that are causing him to hesitate. That will make it easier for him to move towards the solution. The blockage may be somewhere in the family circle. There may be some issue he worries will explode once that agreement is signed. It's easier to avoid responsibility for the blow up by doing nothing in many cases," confirmed Rick.

"So your Abundant Estate approach is a tool to help create governance and communication in the family circle of a family enterprise?" asked Ross.

"It could easily be a part of that model. I focus on the intergenerational wealth-continuity aspect, so I'm not exclusively referring to business families. But, of course, I could build it into family governance in an enterprise scenario. That would include elements such as a family charter or constitution and a formal representative body like a family council," said Rick.

"That's the topic of another day, Rick," laughed Ross. "However, I can see how that can fit in. In a way, you are getting Sarah and Doug started in this with a specific focus on their estate planning."

"Baby steps," smiled Rick.

"So, I was intrigued somewhat by the so-called FISH concept you mentioned at our lunch. Can you tell me more about that?" asked Ross.

"The assets of a family are about a great deal more than the business or other financial assets," added Rick. "They are also about the human, intellectual and social assets of the family."

"Okay, well, that's of interest to me and is why, in part, I wanted to chat today. I am suspicious now that the reason Doug won't do the corporate reorganization as proposed and why he keeps putting it off has something to with concerns about how it will play at home," added Ross. He was visibly excited to know that he may finally be on to the blockage keeping Doug from going forward.

"You think he's looking at the endgame and he doesn't like what he sees. It might save tax, but the human toll is very high—too high. Or even worse, unknown. This is an opportunity to find out what that blockage is and maybe help him manage through it in some way," added Rick.

"I think there are several things at play, really. He has this great business built through entrepreneurship over the years and yet he is risk-averse in the planning. The benefit is so obvious and the tax savings so profound, but we can't move him to decide," bemoaned Ross.

"Most people don't make decisions on numbers, Ross. They need the emotion of a compelling story. Doug needs to have a genuine context for the plan that advances what's most important to him. Do we know yet what is most important?" asked Rick.

"Not yet," sighed Ross. "I think you will find out for all of us as you delve deeper in the estate piece. And this is where you may be able to help me. To use your words, I have worn only one hat with him—two, I suppose, if you include being a friend—for a long time. Putting on another hat this far along is tough. I don't want to learn on the job with my friend and best client. But I know something has to be done. Sarah really liked what you were saying about using the financial assets to invest in the family. That resonated with her," said Ross.

"What about Doug, did it resonate with him much?" asked Rick. He was already convinced it had, based on his own observations. This was a moment of truth. "I think it did . . . a lot. But not in the way you might think, which is the problem, I suppose," said Ross.

Rick sipped on his coffee and thought for a moment before he added, "He's concerned that the business transition will eternally drive away one of the kids, frankly, Kelly. That's interesting, the only reason to worry about that is if—"

Ross interrupted: "Is if that relationship can be saved or, at least, he wants to save it. This is where I get out of my comfort zone. I mean, I am a commercial lawyer. How do I diagnose or deal with this stuff?"

"He could have any commercial lawyer he wants. He keeps you because he trusts you and you might be a linchpin in the solution to his problem," mused Rick.

"Why do you say that?" asked Ross.

"Jim tells me you have a great relationship with Kelly and you work with the business in detail. You are swimming in some special water when it comes to Doug. Maybe he's concerned that finalizing any transition will crystallize the separation from Kelly for all time and he'll lose that opportunity to mend the fence," added Rick. "You know, once the deal is done, your involvement will diminish and that extra connection to Kelly will be lost. Plus, if he sees a wedge in the reorganization plan, he may be fearful that will become permanent. Not making a decision is a way of keeping the lines of communication open. At least through the back channels."

"Maybe. That did occur to me. That's why I think this FISH-y concept you discussed caught their ear," added Ross.

"It's FISH, not so much fishy, but FISH," Rick clarified. "The idea is that the financial assets of a family enterprise, including a business, are servants of the family members and not the other way around. That is to say, the financial wealth is there solely to invest in the human, social and intellectual capital of the various family members. Sustaining the financial wealth over generations is a way to ensure that the family always has the ability to invest in and regenerate its other sources of capital over the long term. Conversely, investing in the intellectual, social, and human capital of the family also helps to sustain and regenerate the financial capital. It's a virtuous circle of inter-generational wealth sustainability."

Ross leaned back and said, "If that's true, it's a very exciting model. But if it isn't true, the worst that has happened is that the family's core goals and fears have been explored and discussed. We tried, and by using this model, we tried harder."

Impressed, Rick shared the chart he had created so that Ross could access the basic definitions. While Ross was reading the materials, Rick grabbed more java to keep the conversation going. He was delighted that this had not been the discussion he was fearing.

As he returned with the coffees, he asked Ross, "I'm curious how this resonated with the two of you. I get Doug, but why you?"

Ross paused and thought for a moment. "Well, simply put, I have seen a few succession scenarios pass across my desk over the years, and when they work, it's great—but when they fail, the damage is spectacular. It's not just the money lost in court, but also the family relationships that are destroyed. I have a daughter about Kelly's age. I can't imagine my life if she were estranged from me. She is the light of my life."

"As you reflect on some of the flame-out successions you encountered, was there a common theme or issue that led to the lawsuits and conflict?" asked Rick.

Ross paused for a moment. He was deep in thought when the waitress, Amy, came over to say hello to Rick.

"Hey, it's crayon boy. How goes the battle, sir?" she laughed as she topped up their Konas.

"Crayon boy?" laughed Ross.

"Please explain, Amy," motioned Rick to Ross.

Amy recounted the story of the monochrome sunflower, including the discussion they'd had about groupthink and the danger of having only one tool in the professional toolkit. After this amusing retelling, Rick took out the picture, which he carried in his briefcase as a reminder and source of inspiration. They all laughed and Amy returned to the front counter.

"That's it!" said Ross.

"What's that?" asked Rick.

"As I reflect on the transitions that failed," Ross began, "I think a common cause of each failure was siloed or monolithic thinking. As professional advisors, we didn't really worry too much about what was actually going on in the family or the business, we were just focused on 'our' crayon—the toolkit of solutions readily available to us from our expert training. We ended up coloring the picture as we wished it to appear and not at all how the client wanted or needed it to appear. It was the tyranny of our expertise at work," he finished.

"You saw only what you were trained to see?" asked Rick.

"That's right," agreed Ross. "And, to add to that, we have an outsized level of confidence in the sureness of our judgment."

"It is a very dynamic and uncertain area," smiled Rick. "Absolute certainty is a rare commodity."

"Yes, but admitting to uncertainty is admitting there is a chance—a good chance—of error. That has implications on what we do, Rick," said Ross. "Clients don't pay for errors."

Rick sat quietly for a moment and then added, "Ross, I am going to write down three numbers. I want you to look at them and write the next two subsequent numbers you think are in the sequence. Then, ask me any clarification questions needed before you tell me what you think the pattern is. Is that okay?" asked Rick.

"Go for it," said a bemused Ross.

Rick wrote down:

3 5 7

Ross thought for a moment and jotted down the next two numbers he expected in the sequence.

"Any questions?" asked Rick.

"Could a following number be an odd number?" Ross asked.

"Yes," responded Rick.

Sensing a trick, Ross asked another question, "Is seventeen a possible number in the longer sequence?"

"Yes," said Rick.

Ross folded his hands and said, "I've got it. The pattern is ascending prime numbers."

Rick smiled and said, "No, it is not."

Ross stared at the three numbers and then reflected on his questions. "It has to be. They are all prime numbers. I saw the ascending pattern and then asked two questions that confirmed that it was the pattern. It has to be the answer."

"The sequence is simply one of ascending numbers. Do you see what you did?" asked Rick.

Ross pondered for a moment and then laughed, "My mind latched immediately onto a pattern and then I only asked questions that proved my own theory. I didn't ask questions that would disprove my theory."

"If you had asked if 8 fit the pattern, you would have been correct as well," said Rick.

"That's a good illustration," said Ross. "As experts, we settle in on what we think we see, because we have been trained to see that, and we don't spend much time testing out other possible explanations."

Rick nodded and said, "It's a human trait," then went on. "It gets worse, actually, because sometimes we strive very hard to see patterns where none exist at all. It's a trick our evolutionary mind uses to make things simple. However, it can lead to terrible outcomes."

"I can see now where feedback in a room from a variety of other professionals can reduce the risk of a fishbowl effect like that on advice and decision-making," Ross shared. "You know, sometimes it's good to imagine the perspective of someone outside the 'bowl' of the family or the business to see things more clearly. Sometimes we take a lot for granted and read things into situations based on past experiences."

"I will use the fishbowl reference to segue a return to the various sources of family capital we were discussing," laughed Rick.

"Huh?" said Ross.

"So the FISH idea would be attractive because it really is different," Rick began. "It puts the full bounty of the family ahead of just the financial bounty. Instead of planning for the financial wealth to transition, do you like the idea that the family should be prepared to receive the financial bounty and that it should be deployed solely to advance their interests?" summarized Rick. "I guess what I am asking is, do you like the Abundant Estate approach?"

Ross smiled and nodded in the affirmative. "I do like it, Rick. We need to understand the family better, I suppose," added Ross, "if we are going to be able to plan for them successfully. Okay, let's discuss this chart a bit."

"Right," started Rick, "everybody pretty much understands financial wealth. Every real estate or business asset, for example, also has a monetary value. I tend to include the business as a financial asset because it generates income and capital growth. Retirement funds, insurance and other savings can be put into this category as well, at least for the purposes of this discussion."

"Okay, so intellectual capital, what is that?" asked Ross.

Rick read the brief summary, "This is about what the family knows, including content and processes associated with sustaining the other forms of wealth. This kind of wealth includes the treasured family stories because they help to define the values and distinctive qualities of the family. Storytelling also promotes intergenerational entrepreneurism. Telling them captures the family's essence and collective wisdom from experiences. In a knowledge-based economy, this may be the most important source of capital. Really, it's about what a family knows about itself and the world in which it operates."

"I have noticed over the years that successful families seem to understand how to do things that work. They understand their history and the lessons from that history. Is that part of it?" asked Ross.

"Yes, and, as I mentioned, there is evidence that storytelling in business families is an important contributor to developing family entrepreneurship. That makes entrepreneurship a vital and renewable resource in a family. In fact, Doug specifically mentioned that he was concerned that his gift, entrepreneurship, would not be sustained after his death. Telling stories is a way to invest in that accumulated intergenerational source of capital. It's a level of know-how that can be passed along and added to inside a family—if it's done purposefully," cautioned Rick.

"Purposefully? I assume you mean that there is a deliberate effort to pass along this intellectual resource. That would imply you can describe, isolate and quantify the asset? You would also need to know how to replicate it so it could be created in areas of the family where it hasn't fully taken root?" thought Ross aloud. His head was clearly spinning a little.

"The purpose behind the planning is a strategic imperative; it is fundamentally goal- and objective-oriented. If you are attempting to drive an identified purpose, then you have likely gone through the exercise of identifying goals and enumerating objectives. At least to some extent, this is required to achieve a purposeful outcome," added Rick.

"I struggle a bit with that. What is a 'purposeful' outcome in this context?" asked Ross.

This conversation with Ross was good for Rick. Bantering with an expert deepened his own understanding of the potential and the limitations of the Abundant Estate model. Ross was a professional colleague and perhaps one of the toughest audiences he would need to face. Rick thought for a moment and then began to answer the question.

"Well, if we think about the word, it has several meanings and connotations. To be purposeful suggests a tenaciousness that is steadfast and constant. Really, you are resolved to do something very specific and assets will be deployed to achieve that outcome," said Rick.

"Go on," said Ross.

"Well, that is fundamentally strategic," said Rick. "That's what strategy is all about: tactically deploying assets to achieve strategies that will further objectives towards goal attainment. The goal of a strategy model is typically not a moving target. It has a quality of constancy or resolve that can stand the test of time, even lasting through multiple generations if the same goals and values are passed along within the family. All the expended effort and asset deployment is to further that goal or series of goals, all the time. It is a relentless and tenacious pursuit of those goals. Put another way, effort and actions are always aligned with the purpose and goals, making for a very efficient deployment of assets and resources that increase the chances of success in attaining the goals and purpose."

"Okay. So let's take the lofty goal of creating wealth that lasts one hundred years. How do FISH and strategy and purpose all play into attaining that goal?" asked Ross.

"Creating long-term wealth that's sustainable for generations is an increasingly important goal. I would have done an initial values exercise and created some form of mission statement for the family. That helps to set the framework of the process. So, let's start by breaking down the phrase a little, just to create a common vocabulary," said Rick.

"Wow, you are a lawyer," laughed Ross.

Laughing as well, Rick started the dissection. "The one-hundred-year wealth idea is a good example of a goal. One starting point or objective is to define the wealth of the family. Dig in to FISH to create an inventory of the family's wealth in all of the areas, not just financial. Then ask which sources are the ones the family wants to see maintained for generations. It's a powerful process and a superb way to build cohesion in the family."

"They must always say they want to preserve financial wealth; that's where people default to, I have to believe," said Ross.

"Almost every time, unless and until we take the time to reveal the other forms of family wealth. Then I tend to see an inversion. Then, the financial is important, but not to the extent that investing in the remainder of the family legacy will be," added Rick.

"So, then you take the audit you conducted on the family's sources of wealth and you tell them, 'Here are some ways we can invest the financial capital into those sources to attain long-term wealth?'" asked Ross.

"I move on to create strategies and tactics to achieve those goals," said Rick. "I should add, one major change you will see is that I don't *tell* people anything. I work to help them identify their own goals and priorities. That's what makes the plan authentic and more likely to last the long term with less conflict and litigation. We are really showing them possible paths to success rather than telling them which to choose. The solutions aren't prescriptive; rather, they are more collaborative and organic. Plus, the very processes created to reveal these priorities—"

Rick was interrupted then by Ross, who said, "The processes create learning and authentic governance, and the family learns to solve their own problems. They still need lawyers and tax advisors and other professionals to bring the plan tactics to life, but it's their own model. That's what would lead to more executed shareholder agreements and estate plans . . . engaged authenticity." The penny was dropping for him.

"Now, social capital is another form of family capital into which financial resources can be invested. Do you have a sense of the concept of social capital?" asked Rick.

"If I had to guess, I would say it is the capital a family creates with their standing in the community or communities to which they belong. That seems a likely definition," added Ross proudly.

"I think that is a great way to define it. I use a definition that highlights relationships between individuals and organizations that facilitate action and create value," said Rick.

Ross thought for a moment and added, "As I reflect on social capital, it seems to me it is mostly experiential. That is to say, you have to get out and build it up for it to happen."

"Yes," said Rick. "I think that's bang on. And to do that, we have to establish networks that allow us to benefit from the laws of attraction. We attract people who are like us; that is, people who are also about investing in the strength of their networks. Since they swim in similar streams, the strength of that network becomes profound and is a force multiplier for everyone involved. It is also about the idea that positivity begets positivity. In this respect, philanthropy is a great way to build social capital while at the same time developing a sense of responsibility to the community and reinforcing the family brand in a positive manner. It also provides great leadership opportunities in the family enterprise," said Rick.

"These other sources of family capital, like social capital, they don't just exist without effort. I would think this requires effort for a family to maintain?" asked Ross.

"I think that's it, Ross. Social capital has a shelf life. Even if it is held dear and cultivated by one generation, it can be very difficult to transfer between generations, unless it is purposefully upheld and lived as a family value and enshrined in the collective goals the family works towards. This is why I like to add the ideas of facilitating action and creating value: involving the entire family in strategies that will sustain social capital, like philanthropy and service to the community, will help to ensure that it will be successfully transferred from one generation to the next. Social capital must be invested in on both sides of the generational ledger or it quickly atrophies. If you aren't growing, you're dying, right?" asked Rick.

"That's called entropy. Everything in nature is dying and then being regenerated. You are proposing to reverse that usually immutable process with purpose. This is exciting. So the action is the process of building the relationships or, at least, of sustaining the existing ones?" asked Ross.

"Yes, and the added value added is clearly the appreciation of the social capital that the family has to draw upon when needed," finished Rick.

"That exercise undoubtedly creates a virtuous circle of self-sustaining social capital," said Ross.

They agreed that the core of a purposeful estate plan would seek to invest with deliberate and strategic purpose into sustaining and growing the family's social, human and intellectual sources of capital. Failing to do that in the wealth-continuity plan dissipates this sort of wealth and future generations lose its potential.

"You know, I have often wondered how to help families avoid the phenomenon where inheritances and family businesses are gone in three generations. Some of my colleagues assume that's unavoidable, and I suppose I always have assumed so as well. But as I reflect on your broader definition of wealth, it may be possible to avoid that old saying . . . what is it now?" searched Ross.

"Shirtsleeves to shirtsleeves in three generations," finished Rick.

"Yes, that's it. Assuming this idea of FISH is correct, investing in the various forms of capital is really a way of growing total family wealth and sustaining it for a long time. We are using the family financial wealth to teach the children and grandchildren how to fish for opportunity rather than rely on having opportunity come to them by chance," added Ross. "Can we discuss the other two sources of family capital?"

"Of all the four types of wealth, I feel human capital is the most profound and maybe the most challenging to manage and develop. This idea sees each person as an individual with value and potential. It's about the inherent worth of each person in the family and the collective value of all family members," said Rick.

"I have seen some terrible situations where families are plagued with drug addictions or other dependencies. Finding worth there is hard, but not impossible," added Ross.

"Well, you are part of the intellectual, social and human capital of the client's lives. You have connections that may be able to help them find the hope and comfort their loved one needs. That has value and most assuredly can precipitate positive action," said Rick.

Ross referred to Rick's table and commented, "I like this part, 'including innate and learned skills and abilities, personality, reputation and credentials.' Everybody has some of those. We all have something to give and dreams to which we aspire. That's very different from what we usually see with trust planning."

"How do you mean?" asked Rick.

"Well, ironically, most trusts I draft reflect a lack of trust. I am trying to keep the financial wealth from being pissed away by an incapable or immature beneficiary. Sometimes the trustees don't even know the beneficiary. How can they understand the needs if they don't know the person?" Ross asked.

"Trusts are an important tactical tool for sure, but that mindset seems kind of hollow and incomplete, doesn't it?" asked a smiling Rick.

Ross pondered for a moment and then somewhat forlornly said, "I wonder if I have been doing this ass-backwards all these years? I always start from the proposition that the financial wealth must be protected from the beneficiaries or just given to them outright and 'damn the torpedoes.' I should be looking at how the financial wealth can be used to bring broader personal abundance to the lives of the various beneficiaries."

"Yes, instead you could work on ways to ready them for their lives, prepare them to inherit financial wealth as stewards rather than mere consumers and allow them to be the best they can be and live the fullest lives possible within their means," said Rick.

Ross went silent. "Most of the time, frankly, the beneficiaries are just a name I insert in the usual spot in the will. I rarely ask too much about them on a deeper level and I never strive to meet and understand them. I mean, that's not always possible, but I never tried even when it was. Moreover, with this model, I see a significant change in how trustees should be appointed."

"How so?" asked Rick, already knowing the answer.

"I often just ask the clients who they want to appoint. If they aren't sure, I describe some of the duties. Most of the duties are things they can hire me, an accountant or a trust company to do," said Ross.

"Those are the bare bones of the role. Since you can hire others to do the work, it's the commodity portion of the role. What isn't a commodity in these situations?" asked Rick.

Ross thought for a moment and then added, "What they can't hire is the trustee's own special relationship with the beneficiaries. If they want the trustees to really understand and know the various heirs, then they need to spend some time on that in advance. Investing in beneficiaries also means investing in the trustee and beneficiary relationship," he tailed off, shaking his head.

"I agree," said Rick. "The trustee and beneficiary relationship is incredibly profound and could last for many years. We should be certain to expend resources in a thoughtful manner to ensure that the trustees selected are part of the investment in the beneficiaries. Not mere commodities but people who will bring value and growth to their lives."

Ross nodded and then checked his watch.

"Shoot, I need to get back to court. Time is money, you know," he said. As he stood, Ross opened his briefcase and took out the financials for Doug's business, his draft shareholder agreement, the draft marriage contract that was never signed, newly drafted wills and powers of attorney and the trust deed for the family trust. He handed them to Rick and said, "Here, before I forget, Doug and Sarah wanted me to share these with you and Jim. Privacy is very important to them. I know you will respect that."

The two lawyers shook hands and, as Ross departed, Rick sat down to text Dave.

Rick:

Okay, I am thru the forest.

He started to pack up and walk back to his office. The sun broke through the clouds as he exited Wendel's. He felt his phone buzz in his pocket and saw that Dave had texted back.

Dave:

Was he there to "Tessio" you?

Rick:

LOL. Maybe. But he cares about the client. Supplied all the docs. He was the gatekeeper and I think I am through the doorway.

Dave:

Real change is possible now. Well done. You are on sacred turf now. Work hard to stay there.

Rick:

Thanks, man.

It had been a good day. Rick agreed with Dave; a breakthrough had been achieved.

Rick decided to walk through the public park next to Wendel's on his way back to the office. The sun was shining brightly and the earthy smell of autumn leaves was starting to fill the air. He reflected on Ross's apparent conversion to the Abundant Estate model with some satisfaction. It was entirely possible that Ross was there to decide whether Doug would proceed any further at all with Rick and Jim. If Rick had stumbled or Ross's mind had been closed to real change in process, failure was a likely outcome. A reason to exit the interaction would have been found and it all would have come to an abrupt end. But it didn't.

At the traffic light on the other side of the park, he glanced to his left and noticed a small, faint rainbow taking form to the east. He smiled and thought to himself, "I gained a colleague in this process, and a valuable one, at that. This work with Doug has reinforced my belief that advisors sense they can do more for clients and are simply seeking a clear path to start that journey. Just as I did when I went to San Diego." The sun was warming the air and Rick decided to take one more lap of the park before heading back to the office.

Chapter 8
The Naked Opus

"Remembering that you are going to die is the best way I know to avoid the trap of thinking you have something to lose. You are already naked. There is no reason not to follow your heart."

—Steve Jobs

"Remember that writing is translation, and the opus to be translated is yourself."

—E.B. White

AFTER MANY ATTEMPTS to get the schedule coordinated, the day for the meeting with Alf, Ross, Rick, Jim, and Doug and Sarah Matthews had finally arrived. At Doug's request, the allotted time was pushed later in the day. He had been very adamant that the start time be later in the afternoon.

Since their first meeting with Rick and Jim several weeks earlier, the Matthews had shared e-mails with Rick and had started trading ideas about the next steps in their interaction. They decided this group meeting would be at a local hotel so that no one would be interrupted by phone calls or drop-in chats for the full two hours they had set aside. It was also neutral ground, which leveled the perceptual playing field among the advisors as to who was in charge and allowed everyone involved to focus on the task at hand.

Rick had brought several copies of his final *Abundant Estate* document, to which he had added one additional element. It seemed appropriate given the meeting today and the path everyone had traveled.

The Abundant Estate

1. Begin a process of having family meetings to address the various topics for your intergenerational wealth planning.

2. Use a meeting cycle to discover and articulate your shared family values.

3. Use a meeting cycle to create a family mission statement based on the shared family values.

4. Utilize a SMRT strategic process:

   a. **S**uccess in the achievement of the mission is made possible by identifying key personal and family goals.

   b. **M**eaning is brought to goals by setting clear objectives to break the big goals down into smaller, achievable steps.

   c. **R**ecipes for action are established when strategies are created to achieve the objectives.

   d. **T**hings that will be done to execute on the strategy are tactics.

5. Assess the professional advisory services needed to support your strategic intergenerational wealth plan and assess the strategic capacities of your current professional advisory circle. Once revealed, take the steps necessary to fill any gaps.

The final item was an effort to recognize that a strategic process may be stillborn if the allied advisory team or a key family stakeholder doesn't engage honestly and supportively. Moreover, there may be skills required to execute the tactics that aren't in the wheelhouse of any of the existing team members. Those gaps need to be identified and bridged.

Bridging gaps meant finding advisors with the following characteristics:

- Self-awareness
- Trustworthiness
- A willingness to act as a servant leader
- Possessing professional skill sets that are deep and broad
- A curiosity for finding alignment with deeply held values of the family

In the event of a gap, the multi-disciplinary team surrounding the client has, as a central task, sourcing these types of prospective advisors for the client to consider. This was another way for the collaborative advisory team to demonstrate value to one another and the family they serve.

The goal of today's meeting was to continue the discovery process and elicit more direct information from the clients, and to secure their buy-in on following the strategic engagement model Rick had created.

Rick had prepared an agenda:

1. Summary of last meeting

2. Update on changes since last meeting

3. A wealth management definition

4. *The Abundant Estate* model for the Matthews family

5. Review of today's efforts, assignment of responsibilities and next steps

6. Next meeting date

The hotel lobby was busy that day because the lobby coffee shop was being renovated. Construction workers mingled with a dozen young girls who were there for a dance competition upstairs. Rick smiled as he watched the odd mix of dust-covered men in hard hats sharing space in line with nine-year-old girls in makeup and their hair in buns, all waiting for their pumpkin-spice lattes.

"It takes all kinds," he laughed to himself as he saw Doug and Sarah politely push through the crowd. Catching their eye, he signaled them to an open space in the lobby and suggested they grab a coffee before heading up to the conference room.

"These girls remind me of my daughter when she was that age. I spent a lot of hours sitting in the car while Kelly was at her dance lessons. I used to read and get organized for the next day. Then, when the weather was warm, we would go for ice cream after dance. I have good memories of those times," said Doug.

"Did Kelly stay in dance? Did she do exams or competitions?" asked Rick. He knew the questions to ask because his daughters also danced.

"She did both and then she taught for years. I think she still does classes at a studio in Kihei," he responded whimsically.

"You are not too sure?" asked Rick as the coffee was poured.

"They don't speak much anymore," said Sarah. "It's a little strained."

"Well, I'm sorry to hear that. I'm sure that isn't easy, and she is so far away, too. That must be a challenge," added Rick.

They took the elevator up in silence. Jim had e-mailed and said he would be late for the meeting. They moved into the conference room that Rick had secured. Alf was already there and he made some small talk with Doug and Sarah. Ross had not yet arrived.

While they waited for Ross and Jim, they settled in and opened up their papers and folios while Rick handed out the proposed agenda.

Rick's iPhone buzzed with an e-mail from Jim saying that Ross would be unable to attend. He was sending his associate, Michelle Russell, in his place. She was already with Jim and they were en route. In the interest of time, they suggested that the meeting proceed with the first few items on the agenda in their absence.

Rick was a little confused that Ross had decided to send his associate. Although Michelle was deeply trusted by Sarah and Doug, he was concerned that Ross's failure to attend signaled that he didn't see particular value in this process. He needed to be vigilant and turn this potential setback into an opportunity to keep pushing forward.

When Rick told the Matthews that Michelle would be attending the meeting instead of Ross, Doug glanced at Sarah, and she seemed oddly unperturbed. Rick was almost certain he caught the hint of a smile on Sarah's face.

They discussed the first two items on the agenda. Rick shared that he had met Ross and they'd discussed the FISH concept in great detail. He showed Sarah the 3-5-7 experiment and she was curious about how that had arisen.

"I find it refreshing that our advisors are capable of sharing their fallibility with one another. Nobody likes a peacock strutting around thinking his poop doesn't smell," she said.

Doug laughed aloud, "Sarah can't stand when egos get too involved. 'They should be checked at the door,' she always says."

Alf added, "True collaboration needs to take place in fertile soil among all parties. This allows things like trust and respect to grow. Poop probably helps that soil though."

Everyone laughed at Alf's attempt at potty humor.

"Sarah, before we move into the third item—developing the actual strategic process—I thought I observed in the first meeting that you were relieved to be moving ahead in this engagement. Is that a fair reading?" asked Rick.

"I was very concerned that this would be a simple-minded discussion about tax planning. I understand that that stuff is important, but I feel the central issues get pushed aside sometimes. Plus, that whole experience with Holistic Financial was so off-putting," Sarah added.

"So, you have some threshold worries and concerns. Doug, can we spend some time on that? I think it will inform the third agenda item," asked Rick.

"Please. Let's start there. I agree," said Doug, without hesitation.

Rick was delighted to see the high level of engagement. "Tell me about what draws you to do this planning," he said to Sarah.

"Rick, I was divorced right after I had Arthur. I spent many years struggling to make ends meet. I had very little help from anyone except my parents. They didn't have much to share, but they did their best," she started.

"Tell me about that time. How old was Arthur?" asked Rick.

"He wasn't even a year old at the time. He was a big change in our lives and we were young; my ex wasn't ready for the responsibilities of life. He basically just ran away. I had to move back with my parents for a while and we lived in their basement. I finished school and then had a job offer out west and took it. Arthur and I went out there and it wasn't easy. I ended up working very long hours. We didn't have much, but we always had each other," she continued.

Doug hung on her every word. He turned and added, "She's a fighter and always has been. Very independent. Arthur is too. He is a top-notch young man. He excels at everything he tries."

Rick smiled and complimented her and Arthur on surviving what must have been a very difficult time. "Lots of people go the other way and it ends badly," he added.

"It could have, but I really think that having so little made us strong. I never had to say, 'I won't do that, Arthur,' because the fact was, I couldn't anyway. Most things were out of reach financially. Arthur was a good student and, with my family's help and scholarships, he flourished. He did it on his own," she added.

"I am sure you and your parents were far more instrumental in his success than you realize. We will get into this more but his success was likely a product of his human capital and your social capital. Can you describe that time a little for me?" asked Rick.

Sarah described a period of incredible financial and emotional strain. She had to work long hours to make ends meet, and her parents took care of Arthur while she fulfilled this obligation. Her father had owned a successful electrical contracting business. Her mother was a retired teacher. They were a resourceful and community-minded couple.

"My dad took Arthur to all of his service club meetings. He'd be out there cleaning cars and collecting donations with all of Dad's friends. My mother would bring him into the school to meet the other teachers and administration staff. Their community became Arthur's. Over time, those connections he had made were very helpful when he needed summer jobs and college references because all of those people helped Arthur to get into a very difficult program in university," smiled Sarah, with a tear visible in her eye.

"As I suspected," added Rick, "that is what is called 'social capital.' We will come to that in this process. That is an asset into which financial assets can be invested to leverage and unleash the growth of human capital. That's what happened for Arthur and, if we are honest, what has helped each and every one of us at some point in our lives."

Everyone briefly shared a story about how someone in their past had helped them get a job, enter a study program, or exit a tricky situation. It was a good moment of bonding for a group of strangers who were evolving into a cohesive team.

"Sarah, can you tell me more about Arthur?" asked Rick. He wanted to keep the momentum going. "Does he have any relationship with his father?"

"Unfortunately," Sarah sighed, "his father passed away several years ago. After we divorced, he decided to grow up and he finished university. Over the years, he eventually became very successful in business and amassed a fair bit of wealth. He never remarried and he left the bulk of the financial legacy to Arthur. Of course, by then, we had endured so much and managed to find our own way. The money worries me a little."

"Can you tell me what concerns you about that situation?" asked Rick.

"Well, frankly, he may never need to work. He gets the bulk of the wealth from a trust over the next few years. I have some fear this will diminish his incentive to grow and learn. That said, he has good values that he learned from my parents and through all the years we struggled. I suppose my greater concern is that our hardship means he will spoil his own children someday," said Sarah.

"So, if I'm hearing you right, Arthur is well-adjusted in his personal relationship to wealth but you are concerned that, being new to this kind of liquid wealth, he will be overly generous to his kids so they don't have to suffer and scrape like you and he did?" asked Rick.

"That's exactly it," sighed Sarah. "I want the legacy of our lives to be positive and not to foster . . . what do you call it when young people are ruined by wealth?"

"Affluenza," said Alf.

Rick asked Doug what he thought of the situation and he was quick to respond, "Well, honestly, good fortune is what came between Kelly and me. She rejected our wealth and it ripped the family apart. So, I appreciate Sarah's concern."

Rick mentally noted that Doug believed his wealth had poisoned his relationship with his daughter. Jim thought it was the polluting that ScrapCo used to perpetrate. It was obvious that promoting better communication was an opportunity to build understanding in this family.

"I would love to meet him someday. Would you consider including Arthur in future meetings, maybe with your children as well, Doug?" asked Rick. "I would like to interview all of the adult stakeholders with your permission?"

They both quickly nodded their assent.

"I'm not flying you to Hawaii for Kelly though," laughed Doug. "That will need to be a technology-based interview."

They all laughed as Rick snapped his fingers and said, "I was too obvious, too obvious."

He continued, "So it's okay if I reach out to Kelly to see if she will take part?" asked Rick. He was a little surprised Doug had intimated that this might be successful.

"It's worth a try," he said. "She may be into it."

Rick turned to Sarah, "I think I may have cut you off there, Sarah. I was excited about the prospect of a trip to Maui. Please go on about Arthur."

"It's interesting," Sarah said. "He is so smart and has been so successful, but he needs to understand the worlds of finance and legal issues a bit better. He's so young and trusting."

Doug added, "I would be happy to have him meet Jim and yourself. It would be good for him. I also think he would appreciate understanding the tax world associated with significant wealth, Alf."

Alf nodded and added that he had worked with many families to create financial literacy programs and experiences for the ascending next generations.

"I feel that is part of building the accountability and stewardship component of wealth," added Alf.

Rick added that building a healthy relationship with wealth was important to ensuring that it is a source of happiness and personal growth in a family rather than a source of guilt, bitterness and negative entropy. It was agreed that this would be the topic of a future meeting.

"I'm curious . . . how does he get along with your children, Doug?" asked Rick.

"Arthur is a very friendly young man. He is like a human bridge—he can connect with anybody. He gets along with them very well. They all get along famously, actually," added Sarah.

Doug sighed a bit and added, "In a strange way, he's been good for my relationship with Kelly. I communicate with her a bit more now and get much more news because Todd, Arthur and Kelly get along so well."

"Doug, can you tell me more about Kelly? I want to understand that relationship," asked Rick.

"She lives in Kihei, Maui, and has been there for many years now. She is married to a really awesome guy named Paul. He is from Hawaii. They met in university and married after graduation. They have two children, Ella and Elsa. Kelly is a researcher for an organic farm. They have vineyards, fish ponds, shrimp ponds and, of course, taro for poi. She is very clever. Just like her mother," described Doug.

"Wait, they have vineyards in Hawaii?" asked Alf.

"Now that's a wine tour I want to take," interjected Rick.

"She is very successful and well regarded in her field. They have a great life and will never leave," added Sarah.

Everyone in the room laughed and agreed that there would have to be a pretty substantial reason for ever leaving Hawaii.

"You noted that the relationship was strained but has evolved since you married Sarah. Can you tell me about that?" asked Rick.

"Kelly is a lot like her mom. She is strong, intelligent and purposeful in how she lives her life. She is a staunch environmentalist," started Doug.

"She hates that Doug runs ScrapCo. She thinks we pollute and destroy the environment," explained Sarah.

"Well, in fairness, we used to, but we're better now. I am more of a recycler these days. My first wife was also uncertain about how ethical the old business was. I just made money, I wasn't too interested in how I got there. But after Gabrielle got cancer, Kelly was sure the business had somehow been at fault or that there had been bad karma or whatever. It was a really tough time. I had no energy, between dealing with Gabrielle's illness, running a growing business and fighting with Kelly. I said stuff, she said stuff. It was bad. I haven't personally had a lot of contact, but, as I said, the kids all stay in touch," continued Doug.

"How is your relationship with Kelly?" asked Rick of Sarah.

"Strangely enough, while it was frosty at first, she e-mails me photos of Ella and Elsa. I think she does it to share with Doug," said Sarah.

They discussed Kelly's situation a little more. It was clear that Doug and Sarah wanted to have a relationship with her. Rick felt Kelly was reaching out for greater connection as well. It seemed possible that Kelly was more like her dad than her mother, but he decided to keep that to himself for now.

"It's a blessing that the kids get along. I am not a family psychologist or therapist, Doug, but it sounds like you and Kelly both want to communicate but need to find some common ground. She's sending photos to Sarah, which is a huge step. This may be one of the moments in life when you extend the olive branch," added Rick. "But maybe get some input from a family therapist first. I know a really good one I have worked with and she may be able to give you some advice on your own approach to the situation. Not so much to manage Kelly, but to understand her view and how she might see things. You know, to gain perspective."

"I would like that very much. I am not getting any younger and I would love to be a bigger part of Ella and Elsa's lives. I have only two grandchildren right now. I would really like that . . . but I didn't expect to talk about all this stuff. I thought we were just doing estate planning," added Doug.

"This is all part of the strategic approach I'm proposing that we apply to your transition planning," explained Rick. "But most people don't get to this level at all. Primarily because the will is viewed as a one-off commodity, as the entire estate plan in and of itself, rather than just one step in a much bigger and more comprehensive process. How can we plan if we don't first understand the dynamics of the situation?"

"Can I fill Rick in a little on Todd before the others arrive?" asked Alf.

They all nodded and Rick glanced at Sarah and Doug as Alf proceeded to explain Todd's situation. He observed some apparent angst on Sarah's face as the topic of Todd's new girlfriend, Wanda, was discussed.

When Alf finished, Sarah added, "She's been married before . . . twice. And she has a little one from another relationship."

"May I ask if Todd's relationship with Wanda is partly what's driving your enthusiasm to get started in this process?" asked Rick. "Are you concerned that this new relationship may complicate the family dynamics and the planning you do?"

"Please don't get me wrong, she's very nice and all, but we don't really know her and Todd is an uncomplicated guy," said Sarah with genuine concern.

"Okay then. So Wanda's appearance on the scene is a little wake-up call that maybe things need to be reviewed. They're just dating, or are they living together?" asked Rick.

"They are getting pretty serious and have been talking about living together. Nothing more serious yet though," added Sarah.

"Well, that is helpful because it leaves us some runway space for planning. It will be delicate, but that's family and business—very fluid and dynamic," said Rick. "At some point in this process, we will discuss the three-circle model and how we can use it to manage the more challenging aspects of the intersection of the family members and their needs with the requirement of running and owning your family business."

Doug commented that he and Ross had discussed the concept after his meeting with Rick at Wendel's. "Ross seemed intrigued by that model as a way to gain the perspective of others and thereby better manage the various dynamics."

Rick looked at Doug and said, "You have really come around to be fully engaged in this process. I am as excited as I am surprised. What made the difference? I mean, we haven't even talked tax, which I had been repeatedly warned was your favorite subject."

Doug laughed gently as he started to respond, "Well, initially as we started this process . . . well, frankly, it seemed like a load of crap to me. I had talked with Ross and he said it was airy-fairy, touchy-feely work that I wouldn't like and didn't need. I was here because Sarah wanted it and she seemed intrigued. I figured if I just went along, eventually it would run out of gas and stall. I am not a big guy on change when I can't see the outcome. I was gabbing about our meeting at work and Todd started to wonder who was pushing for the changes and what the changes were going to be. I felt a lot of pressure, which was stupid. Todd and I had a fight and it was tense for a little while," said Doug.

"Oh," said Rick. "I am so sorry. Look, this is your process, we can stop anytime if you feel this is too stressful."

"No," added Sarah. "Tell them what happened next."

"I have permission to shed a little light here," added Alf. "Todd is also my client. He called me and wanted to know what was up. That was the day we all had lunch with Ross, so I completely understood where this was likely heading and I explained what was really happening."

"He apologized the next day," said Doug. "But, the reality was, it was me who needed to apologize. I was moping around and speaking ill of you and the whole process. . . ."

"Whaaaat?" squealed Rick.

Doug and Sarah laughed.

"That was my point. You were only the messenger. I needed to hear the message. I wasn't sharing important information at work and I realized things needed to change. Todd and I spent some time over dinner and he sort of spilled his guts that he loved working at ScrapCo and wanted to own it someday. However, he had seen what happened with Kelly and me, and he didn't want to jeopardize his relationship with his sister. He saw all these lawyer and accountant meetings being set up and he was concerned that I was just doing things without his input. He had no idea what the hell was going on anywhere. He is totally invested career-wise with the company and was getting uneasy that choices I was making would affect his life in some dramatic way," added Doug.

"That's when Doug realized that his old ways of making decisions and communicating with the family were not good enough anymore. He needs to change. He needs to be more open about his ideas and planning goals. It won't be easy for him, but he has to try," said Sarah.

Rick decided to act on a hunch and asked, "Did Todd call Kelly through all of this? They seem to have a good relationship."

"Actually, yes," interrupted Alf. "And then she called Ross and they had a very long conversation. I guess they always had a special

connection and she knew how much Doug trusted him and he had
been their friend and lawyer for so many years. He discussed your
strategic approach with her, and she was totally on board. Her exact
words were to the effect that some sunlight and conversation would
be awesome for the family."

There was an awkward silence, then Rick spoke up, "Well, usually I have to actually *do* something before the shit hits the fan, so
this is a pleasant change."

They all chuckled.

Rick continued, "This is likely a moment we don't want to miss,
Doug. I think that's why you are here in full readiness to start this
process. You want it as much as Kelly and Todd do . . . and, frankly,
Sarah."

Doug smiled and nodded in agreement.

"I am sorry that Ross couldn't attend," said Rick. "But I think
he has moved this process dramatically forward in some mysterious
manner."

"He could have been here," Sarah interjected, looking up from
her smartphone. "He wanted Michelle to take this over. She will be
here through it all after he has retired. I love her energy and her
spirit for holistic planning and the fact that she wants to be engaged.
Ross insisted that she be allowed to proceed in his place."

The stars were aligning, so Rick pushed forward into the agenda. "All right," he began. "Let's go back to item number three, the
Abundant Estate model. This model has been evolving as I have been
working with all of your advisors. We are all confident it will work
well for your situation. But, do you remember in our first meeting I
asked you to consider the statement 'I plan for my family'? There was
some homework I gave you at the end of that meeting. I wanted you
to consider the phrase and what it means to you."

Just then, Jim and Michelle entered the room with profuse apologies. The city was bisected in many places by nineteenth-century
rail lines that were never moved as the city grew. As a result, long
freight trains were constantly snarling traffic. It was part of living in
this city. They all laughed as Jim advised that he had been slowed by

a "Seinfeld" train. He called it that because no fewer than fifty of the rail cars he and Michelle had to watch pass by were actually empty. They had in fact been delayed by nothing.

Alf caught up Michelle and Jim on where they were in the meeting.

"If I may, I thought about that statement, Rick," said Jim. "I thought about it in terms of the journey I have been taking with you and these clients. As an advisor, my most sacred task is to ensure that the steps I take on behalf of my clients are always *for* my clients—appropriate for their specific situation and purpose, and not simply an off-the-rack, boilerplate solution that's given to them. And by clients, I have come to appreciate that this means the entire family system, not just the people who are hiring me and paying me to do the planning. In this case, the clients are Doug, Sarah, Kelly, Todd, Arthur, their spouses and partners and the next generation. To plan 'for' them, I must understand them and how the dynamics of their family enterprise work. I need to know their values, mission statement and strategic goals before I can do much that's of value. I cannot allow tactics to be deployed until I am at one with the purpose behind planning for this family's enterprise wealth."

There was a hush in the room. Suddenly, Alf started a slow, rhythmic clap and all joined in. It was agreed by all the advisors around the table that they accepted that proposition as the baseline for planning for these clients within the professional limits of their craft.

"Sarah, what about you?" asked Rick.

"We discussed this as well. The only way Jim, Alf, Michelle and you, Rick, can truly help us is if we allow ourselves to be revealed. We need to peel back the onion and let our advisors see the whole picture of our situation before we plan. We also need to define our true wealth—that is, all aspects of our wealth—and plan to sustain that wealth for the long-term benefit of our family. We aren't planning now simply to move assets; we are planning to prepare our heirs to receive, enjoy, grow with and steward our total enterprise wealth," said Sarah.

The room clapped for Sarah. Rick was thrilled that there was consensus on what planning needed to look like to be successful in the long term.

The discussion continued and Doug and Sarah were excited to start with a family-values exercise that would culminate in the creation of a family mission statement. This would logically become the basis for a strategic plan for the family's intergenerational wealth transition. They would work on it at a facilitated family meeting over the Thanksgiving holiday. Jim had been leading the discussions and agreed to arrange the timelines and help the Matthews coordinate all the necessary steps. Rick marveled at how far everyone had come.

Doug was soaking it all in and enjoying the banter of his professional team working together so closely for his family's collective well-being.

"You know," Doug interjected, "this whole process, this strategic approach, it's like we are writing the story of our family. We are collating all the best aspects to create a mission statement and then we will move ahead on the strategy creation. It's going to be a significant body of work."

"A life's work, really. Your family opus," added Jim.

They moved into the next sections on the agenda, including Rick's definition of wealth management. Everyone understood the definition better as they moved into a deeper discussion of the Abundant Estate model.

The discussions and explanations went on for over an hour. During the conversations, Rick had noticed Doug occasionally checking his phone and then tapping away in answer to some message. He often looked up and asked a very pointed question with great animation. The incoming texts made him smile on several occasions.

"Are you texting work?" Sarah finally asked.

Sheepishly, Doug replied, "No, I've been texting some of this to the kids as it has been going on."

"Which kids?" asked a very surprised Sarah.

"Arthur and Todd," he started.

"What about Kelly? She should be in on this, too," said Sarah.

Doug smiled, "She is, that's why I wanted the later meeting, so she could be looped in. They are several hours behind us, you know."

A tear was visible in Sarah's eye. Doug had decided to use this process to make real change, or at least try for it.

"She's coming for Thanksgiving?" asked Sarah.

"They all are, or we can meet them there. I hear it's nice in Hawaii that time of year. Hey, I noticed you were texting earlier as well, what was that all about?" asked Doug with a smile.

"I was just e-mailing Alicia at Holistic Planning to close their file. We won't be needing their services anymore," said Sarah, smiling at Jim, who was visibly pleased.

They agreed to part for the day. They had accomplished a lot and it was time to start documenting their values, goals and wishes and developing a strategic process to bring it all to life. Doug and Sarah agreed to trade e-mails and phone calls with Jim, Rick, Alf and Michelle as they discussed their values and goals and fleshed out their thinking around them. The next appointment was set for thirty days hence to keep the ball rolling.

Doug left first to bring up the car. On her way out the door, Sarah pulled Rick aside and said quietly, "Thank you for this. Doug is a businessman but a family man first. He forgets that sometimes. This discussion has made me more confident than ever that our modern family will be successful."

"You took the first steps, and I think he is ready," said Rick. "There will be bumps along the way because old habits die hard for advisors and clients. Plus, some of the conversations will be intense and raise thorny issues. There may be some pushback against the strategic, purpose-driven approach we're taking," he warned her.

"Well, we're ready for that now if it happens. We have decided to be advocates for our own planning. We know what we want now and this process will add tremendous clarity to our desires. We have a sense of what the priorities need to be. I am so excited for the family meeting during Thanksgiving. What do you call this type of planning if I want to google it?" asked Sarah.

"I would search 'purposeful estate planning,'" advised Rick. "You will find starting points there. I'll send you some great links."

"You know, I have a feeling that going through this process will feel really creative. There is almost an artistry to it when it's done right, I suspect," added Sarah.

As the elevator doors closed, Rick thought about the idea of purpose-driven planning. The only way this approach works, he mused, is if people are prepared to peel off the veneer a little and let others—advisors and family members—help them to paint the complete estate-planning picture authentically. They had to get a little naked and show some vulnerability. It really was a complex undertaking that benefited from the wisdom of many diverse disciplines and perspectives. Best of all, purposeful planning was a collaborative effort, a truly creative process that unfolded and evolved over a long period of time. A purpose-driven estate plan could be seen as a life's work. A life's passion, a naked opus.

Epilogue
A World of Abundance

"When I think about creating abundance, it's not about creating a life of luxury for everybody on this planet; it's about creating a life of possibility. It is about taking that which was scarce and making it abundant."

—Peter Diamandis

TWO WEEKS LATER, Jim poked his head into Rick's office and said, "I have a present for you, to show my thanks for all the work with Doug and Sarah."

"Well, I love presents. Bring it on!" said Rick. Hoping for tickets to a Matthews family retreat in Maui, he was instead given a pound of pure Hawaiian Kona coffee. "This is amazing, Jim, many thanks. Upon reflection, how do you feel about this process now?" he asked Jim.

"It has opened my eyes, Rick. I didn't share with you all the conversations I had with Ross and Doug. In the very beginning, they were very nervous about the process and about the road we were going down with the whole Matthews family," said Jim.

"Were they really that worried?" Rick asked.

"At first they were totally scared. I was, too. I nearly pulled the plug twice on this," he said.

"Why didn't you? Why go ahead and take the risk?" asked Rick.

"I just sensed this was the right way to go," said Jim. "Frankly, I reflected on my own planning in the context of our engagement with Doug. My will is twenty years old. I have accumulated a decent amount of wealth and I have children and grandchildren. I just started asking myself, 'What have I done for my own family? How will they remember me?' You know, what was the whole purpose of growing this, or any, wealth at all?"

"And?" asked Rick.

"My family, Rick. I do this for my family. Ten years ago I had a heart attack at my desk. You know the first thing I saw when I regained consciousness?" asked Jim.

"I doubt it was your money," smiled Rick.

"Exactly; it was my two daughters, because my wife had been traveling abroad with her mother," he said.

"Life is a circle in some ways," added Rick.

"And circles don't break, they go on," said Jim. "That was all I could think of as we went through this planning process with Doug. I need to strengthen those bonds, not weaken them. I need to invest in my family and not just passively leave them with a lump of cash and a pro forma will. Doug and I aren't so different," he added. "The facts are divergent and so is the magnitude of the wealth involved, but the imperatives are the same. We both love our families above all else."

"I'm learning from you now," laughed Rick.

Jim laughed too and suggested it was about time.

"It could still be a bumpy ride for Doug," added Rick. "Is everybody ready for that?"

"We shall see. I just feel better about my involvement. I feel so much more engaged, and I know the clients are too. Doug calls me now with lots of different questions, and so does Sarah. I am much more connected to them and their family. It will be hard to achieve that with all my clients," said Jim.

"Yes, but you'll get there. Some people will really want this approach. Others won't be ready. It's a practice-management mindset. It's also a continuum. You can have a family meeting over a kitchen

table at dinner rather than jetting off to Hawaii for a family conference, if that's the real deal for the family. Crafting the strategic goals
for a family doesn't require immense financial wealth; it simply demands a sense of purpose. In some ways, the less you have, the more
strategic you need to be to achieve your goals," finished Rick.

Nodding in agreement, they shook hands. Jim thanked Rick
again for sharing his new strategic model and giving him new purpose, and not only in his planning with clients. Rick smiled as he
realized that Jim had started the same journey he himself had been
on for some time.

Just then, Rick's phone buzzed—it was Dave Milne texting. He
had been away on vacation for two weeks and was curious about
what had transpired.

Dave:
Sooooo . . . ?

Rick:
The lawyer, accountant and advisor are all on the same
page—my page!

Dave:
The client?

Rick:
Everybody

Dave:
U have resurrected my faith in humanity

At that moment, Liz Stowe, the advisor from down the hall who had
approached Rick about working with a couple of her clients some
time ago, poked her head in the door and said, "Rick, can we speak?
Do you remember Carol and Mark Gumble? They really need to meet.
They are updating their wills and won't be working with the same
legal advisor. They want some help and asked for you specifically
before they got started."

Rick certainly did recall the Gumbles, and still with some regret.
In his eyes, their first meeting was a failed engagement. In some

ways, Carol Gumble reminded him of Sarah; she had a similar gleam in her eye when they touched on the possibilities for broader, more purposeful planning. But Rick's ideas about strategic estate planning had not been fully developed when he met the Gumbles, and their lawyer was firmly stuck in the old way of doing things.

Rick had maintained a level of regret about how he first engaged this couple, knowing that there was unfinished business between them. He was pleasantly surprised by Liz's request to rekindle the conversation with them, now that he was better equipped to advise them. He was convinced that his new Abundant Estate process could help them get more creative in their planning. Together, they could reveal the Gumbles' true purpose and plan to achieve it. He had a chance to turn this failed engagement into a happy ending, and to show the Gumbles the way to create their own purposeful family legacy.

Coming back to earth, he made plans with Liz to connect with the Gumbles in the next few weeks to start a planning engagement. It was a second chance for all of them to get it right.

When he finished with Liz, Rick texted Dave:

Rick:

LOL. Sorry, had to respond to a work request. On to the next client.

Dave:

This time with purpose.

Rick:

From now on, every single time with purpose.

Endnotes

Chapter 1

1 Robert Frost, "The Road Not Taken."

Chapter 4

1 Richard Koch, *The 80/20 Principle: The Secret to Achieving More with Less* (Crown Business, 2008), 142.

2 Harvard Business Review, *On Strategy* (Harvard Business Review Press, 2011), 20.

3 "Things that matter most must never be at the mercy of things that matter least." Johann Wolfgang von Goethe.

Chapter 5

1 Cass Sunstein and Richard Thaler, *Nudge: Improving Decisions about Health, Wealth, and Happiness* (Yale Unversity Press, 2008).

Chapter 7

1 See James E. Hughes, *Family Wealth: Keeping It in the Family* (Bloomberg Press, 2003).

2 Jean-Luc Arregle, Michael A. Hitt, David G. Simon and Philippe Very, "The Development of Organizational Social Capital: Attributes of Family Firms," *Journal of Management Studies* 44:1 (January 2007).

Acknowledgments

The process of conceiving, crafting and writing *The Naked Opus* has been one of the greatest creative experiences I have ever enjoyed. The act of writing this type of book challenged me to understand my own core beliefs and look for solutions to pain points I wanted to resolve.

It was written in my spare time over a lengthy duration, punctuated by delays caused by transitions in my own life and family. Throughout that process my editor, Karen Milner, kept me focused, speaking in a singular voice and with a consistent vision. Her kind hand-holding got this book into your hands.

Many thanks to the cover designer, Adrian So, for finding great images to complement the ideas of the book. Also, thanks to copy editor Lindsay Humphreys for translating my words and punctuation into English. I shouldn't have skipped those classes in high school.

I would also like to thank John Mill for the hours upon hours of coffee and conversation we have had over the years, processing some of these ideas about family wealth planning. Along the way, I have shared my ideas and chapters with many friends and colleagues who offered suggestions for improvement or just plain encouragement. They include Tom Deans, Carol Foley, John Neretlis, Murray Flanagan, Tamelynda Lux, Carol Fickling, Jonathan Creaghan, Mary Bart, Dorothy Swan, Loretta Biscaro Smith, Nathalie Boutet, Diane Silva, Rebecca Griffith, Nicole Bendaly and Steve Legler.

Last but not least, unending thanks to my girls, Hannah, Adelaide and Jennifer for putting up with frequent comments like, "I'll cut the lawn after I edit this chapter," and, "I'd love to do it but I have a deadline." No excuses now, onward and upward.

Mahalo

Public Speaking and Additional Copies

One of my sincere pleasures over the many years of my career has been the opportunity to speak frequently to various groups on the subjects of wealth continuity and business transition planning. The questions, concerns and conversations from many of those events are revealed through the characters in this book.

The Naked Opus: Growing Your Family Wealth for the Long Term is intended for families of wealth and all of their advisors, including:

- Investment advisors
- Accountants
- Lawyers
- Insurance advisors
- Private bankers
- Family business advisors
- Philanthropic professionals
- Executive coaches
- Peer advisory chairs
- Family office professionals
- And many other trusted advisors who serve their clients with purpose and expertise

If you are a member of a family of wealth or a business family, or if you advise these valued clients, and want to learn more about booking Chris Delaney, please contact info@nakedopus.com

You may purchase additional books in paperback or as an e-book by visiting www.nakedopus.com

About the Author

Chris Delaney, B.A., LL.B., B.Ed., TEP, FEA, is an author and keynote speaker. He earned his Bachelor of Laws degree from Western University in 1989 and a Bachelor of Education degree in 1995 from the University of Windsor. He has a Family Enterprise Advisor designation from the Institute of Family Enterprise Advisors (IFEA). He is also a member of the Society of Trust & Estate Practitioners which is the leading international organization for trust and estate professionals. He is also a member of the Law Society of Upper Canada and the Purposeful Planning Institute in Denver, Colorado.

Chris is a frequent speaker on strategic family wealth planning and business transition planning in such diverse locations as London, England; Calgary, Alberta; Toronto, Ontario; Ann Arbor, Michigan; and Montreaux, Switzerland. He has spent the last thirteen years as a lawyer working with families of wealth to create thoughtful and purposeful estate and business succession plans.

Chris lives in London, Ontario, with his wife and two daughters, where he is actively planning his Hawaiian retirement. He hopes to live long enough to see the Toronto Maple Leafs win another Stanley Cup.